2/20/18

Best
Success!

POWER Principles *For Success*

Published by CelebrityPress®, Orlando, FL

CelebrityPress® is a registered trademark.

Printed in the United States of America.

ISBN: 978-0-9907064-1-0
LCCN: 2014951039

This publication is designed to provide accurate and authoritative information with regard to the subject matter covered. It is sold with the understanding that the publisher is not engaged in rendering legal, accounting, or other professional advice. If legal advice or other expert assistance is required, the services of a competent professional should be sought. The opinions expressed by the authors in this book are not endorsed by Celebrity Press® and are the sole responsibility of the authors rendering the opinion.

Most CelebrityPress® titles are available at special quantity discounts for bulk purchases for sales promotions, premiums, fundraising, and educational use. Special versions or book excerpts can also be created to fit specific needs.

For more information, please write:
CelebrityPress®
520 N. Orlando Ave, #2
Winter Park, FL 32789
or call 1.877.261.4930

Visit us online at: www.CelebrityPressPublishing.com

POWER Principles *For Success*

VOLUME **2**

CELEBRITY PRESS®
Winter Park, Florida

CONTENTS

CHAPTER 1

SEVEN STEPS TO ACHIEVE MASSIVE SUCCESS IN BUSINESS!

BY COLIN SPRAKE

One of the most important parts of life is understanding what it takes to be successful. There are many factors that make up success, but there are only a few basic fundamentals to me that have aided in my success, and that are what I consider to be Power Principles. This chapter will take you through how to be massively successful at anything that you do. Just make sure you follow the steps in sequence and enjoy - massive success is on its way!

STEP 1: LIVE ON PURPOSE RATHER THAN OBLIGATION

Firstly, you must have passion and purpose in what you do every day. You have to wake up knowing and feeling on purpose. This took me a long time to realize and figure out. There are many people who exist or live life because of obligation every day, and do the same routine day after day, and never achieve the results that they want. Conversely, there are those who find their purpose and go out and change the world.

The most successful brands on the planet started out with a purpose, and then became massive money makers, not the other way around. Take Apple, Starbucks, Make Your Mark Training & Consulting,

Microsoft: They all started out with a purpose, and the money, success and fame came as result of starting the business with a purpose. Apple wanted to change the world by challenging the *status quo* every time; Starbucks wanted to give people a unique coffee experience; Make Your Mark wanted to inject soul into business and Microsoft wanted to ensure that people could do things more simply and easier with their products. All these companies thrive because of a purpose to help the world and make a difference. So ask yourself the key question, "Am I in business to make a difference or purely for the money?" In my business, we live by the mantra, "When you focus on dollars you will have money to count, and when you focus on people you will have countless dollars."

Finding your purpose is sometimes considered one of the most difficult things in life. We have been taught in most developed societies to go get educated at school, go to college, get a job, go to work and pay taxes. This creates a society of lemmings going out every day doing mostly what they don't want to do in order to make a living. The majority of people get in a car to go to work every day, spend one to two hours going to a place they do not truly like or resonate with, do a job to make money, then jump in their car, return home and repeat the same process for five or six days a week for a number of years. Typically, there is little joy or satisfaction in this type of existence.

On the other hand, when you live on purpose every day, as I do, you feel that sleep is overrated because going to bed interrupts your day. You awake each day with a bounce in your step ready to go to assist your clients. My purpose is to assist business owners and entrepreneurs to be massively successful. There is nothing that drives me more than receiving communications from clients saying that their business has skyrocketed because of our *7-step Business Success System.*

My definition of living on purpose is doing something that you absolutely love, which feels effortless, and is something you would do even if you were not paid to do it, because you love what it does for other people.

STEP 2: RESONATE WITH YOUR GOALS

In order to be massively successful in your business, you must determine what you are targeting or aiming for. You must create a vision for your business. Whether you are a solopreneur or a business with multiple employees, you have to have a vision typed out and put up on a wall in your office, for where your business is going. The vision is the big picture and where you want to be in the grand scheme of things. When you first start out in business, I am a firm believer that you should have a one year plan and a five year vision. Most business owners do not have a vision for their business, and in fact, most business owners plan their vacations in more detail than they plan their businesses!

Having no vision for your business is equivalent to having your entire family sitting in the fully-loaded car waiting to go on vacation, locking up your house, jumping in the driver's seat, having your spouse ask where you are going and you say "on vacation." This means that you could be going anywhere! This scenario describes most business owners on a daily basis: They wake up and do business without a destination in mind. You cannot go on vacation without knowing where you are going and the mode of transport that you are going to use to get there, nor can you do so in your business. When you type out your vision and put it up in a prominent place, it allows your spouse, team, employees, clients and vendors to know where you are going so that they are able assist you with fulfilling your vision.

The most important part of creating your vision is ensuring that you resonate with the end goal. This keeps you on target and does not allow you to be distracted by bright, shiny objects. Many business owners often chase other opportunities or change businesses because they do not have an end goal with which they resonate. This is the most important part of any business plan which will keep you focused and on track to achieve your desired result.

Once you have the vision for your business created and written down, you can then add your mission, which is the step-by-step process for fulfilling your vision. A business with a vision that takes no action operates on hallucination, and a business with a ton of action and no vision is clueless!

STEP 3: DESIGN A PLAN

Once you have a vision for your business that you completely resonate with, I recommend writing down your plan to achieve your vision. If you are just starting out in business, always begin with a business plan which focuses on the next twelve months. Ideally you want a five year vision, but start with a one year plan, because within your first year your business is guaranteed to morph into something that you did not exactly envision, which is good. I am a big fan of one-page business plans to help your business grow. If you'd like to learn how to do this easily, I can help you.

Remember, a business plan guides you along the journey to achieving your vision. It is like a road map or itinerary for your vacation. You cannot go on vacation without knowing where you are going and how you are going to get there. It is the same for your business, you must have a vision you resonate with and a plan that you can action to ensure you fulfill your vision.

STEP 4: GROWING YOUR KNOWLEDGE

I wish we were born with every bit of knowledge that we need to be successful, but we are not. You need to continually grow your knowledge by learning from others who have achieved what you want to achieve. The powerful part about learning from others is that it saves you a ton of time and money – you do not have to make the same mistakes! There are many trainers and educators out there who can assist you; the critical part is to find the ones who have achieved success in the areas you are looking for advice. I personally have mentors assisting me to grow to the next level of success, and I change them every now and again to bring on new mentors who have gone to even greater levels of success.

The challenging part I have both seen and experienced with people is that they ask for advice and attend seminars and trainings, yet they do not implement what they have learned. Implementation of what you have learned is vitally important. Otherwise, you are just wasting your time and money. I have a formula that I like to use; whatever the duration of the training, ensure you put the same amount of time aside after it to implement all the new knowledge, strategies and systems. For example, if you go on a three-day course, put aside the three days immediately after the course to implement everything.

STEP 5: HOLDING YOURSELF ON COURSE

This is a vital part to getting the results you want and to achieving your vision for your business. You must find a group of like-minded business owners who can assist you with staying on track. Being a business owner can be extremely lonely and sometimes daunting, because you may not have a team around you to ask questions and receive good solid answers to grow your business. In fact, many business owners are embarrassed that their business is not truly making the money that they want, so often they do not discuss it with their spouse or significant other. We are all in business to make a difference in the world and make money, but doing it alone is not the easiest and quickest way to achieve your vision. Seek out business accountability groups, like B.E.S.T. Mindset, which work specifically with entrepreneurs, to ensure you achieve the success you want and the support that you are looking for.

STEP 6: CELEBRATION, ACKNOWLEDGEMENT & RECOGNITION

This is probably the most neglected step in the entire process, and yet it is one of the most important. I live by universal principles, which dictate that what you put out there is what you get back. Therefore, when you acknowledge and celebrate your successes, the Universe gives you more to celebrate about. I advise creating a daily habit whereby you celebrate what you achieved the day before to keep you on track and to get you into the habit of celebrating. Even the smallest of successes need to be celebrated to continue to put out into the Universe that you want more to celebrate - and guess what - it always delivers!

It is also essential to recognize your daily achievements and write them down. You will soon start to see that a bunch of small daily successes turns into massive recognition and acknowledgement for what you have achieved. You will be amazed what you have achieved on a monthly basis when you write them down daily.

STEP 7: GROW PERSONALLY

I live by the principle that until you grow personally, it is not easy to grow professionally. Simply put, the more you work on yourself and expand your mindset, the quicker and more easily you will grow your business. One of the most common things I say is, "Business is really simple, until you add human beings!" Yes, we make things extremely complicated. So, I encourage you to keep working on yourself and attend personal development workshops to increase your awareness about you. You will realize that the biggest challenge in your business is the way you think. The quicker you shift your thinking, the sooner your business will achieve massive levels of success!

BONUS STEP: PRINCIPLES I LIVE BY

I often get asked, "Colin, what is the number one principle that has contributed to your massive success?" It is a very simple answer: I've followed and continue to follow all of the above steps, and I never give up until I've achieved my goals. I do not let anything get in my way.

Hurdles or challenges are opportunities to learn and I always ask the question, "What am I meant to learn from this situation?" I take the learning, move on, and continue to implement. I am results focused and not excuse poisoned. I am always asking, "How can I?" versus saying "I can't!"

Most of all I do not overthink everything! My process is to think, make a decision and take action with urgency – *there is no grass that grows under my feet!*

About Colin

Colin H.A. Sprake is a heart-centered Business Sherpa, author, speaker, trainer and creator of The Ultimate Business Success System...with SOUL! – a 7-Step System to $10k profits per month or more, in 12 months or less – SUCCESS GUARANTEED.

A South African native and serial entrepreneur with decades of experience building multiple million-dollar businesses globally in various industries and economies, Colin founded Make Your Mark Training & Consulting in 2004 with a passion to assist entrepreneurs to realize their full revenue and profit potential, and do it with heart -- making a positive impression on those their business impacts: staff, colleagues, vendors, families and the community.

Colin has built Make Your Mark Training on the core values of trust, respect for the individual, unconditional gratitude, integrity, openness to possibilities and commitment to excellence. He also places people above profits.

Colin's conscious business philosophy coupled with his results-driven business success system of live events, group accountability programs and online trainings have created a vibrant, mutually supportive 15k+ community of entrepreneurs in the Vancouver, BC area in Canada within 50km of Colin's home, which is a rarity in the training industry. Duplication and expansion are currently underway for Make Your Mark in Calgary, AB and other key markets in North America and beyond.

Colin is also the author of the #1 Bestseller: *Entrepreneur Success Recipe – The Key Ingredients That Separate The Millionaires From the Strugglers* and the #1 Bestseller: *Stand Apart* co-authored with Dan Kennedy. Colin's articles and interviews have appeared in many local and international print media including *The Globe and Mail, Vancouver Sun, Seattle Times* and *Reno Gazette.* Colin has also appeared on many channels as a guest business expert: Global, MSNBC and CTV to mention a few.

A highly sought after keynote speaker and trainer, Colin guarantees his audiences will walk away from his presentations, no matter how long or short, with practical tools and strategies they can use immediately in their lives and businesses – to achieve greater success and make a positive impact in the world. He also teaches that success is attainable in both family and business without sacrificing one for the other.

Colin currently resides in South Surrey, British Columbia, Canada with his beautiful wife and two daughters. He makes family his #1 priority.

You can connect with Colin at:
Colinea@mymsuccess.com
www.My1PagePlan.com
www.Twitter.com/ColinSprake
www.Facebook.com/ColinSprake

CHAPTER 2

CONTENT IS STILL KING

BY LINDSAY DICKS

Have you ever heard the saying, "Content is king on the Internet?" This statement is true, but it's missing a piece; marketing. Without the marketing aspect, it is like opening the doors to your business and doing no marketing whatsoever. The content is only as good as your marketing. The key behind getting good, qualified traffic is "Content Marketing," or to take it a step further, "personalized, targeted Content Marketing."

So what is **Content Marketing?** And better yet, what is **personalized, targeted Content Marketing?** Content Marketing is simple but can be easily forgotten. It's based on two definitions, content, which is really just information about your particular niche, and marketing, which is the distribution and promotion of that information. In the business world, this means information created and targeted to your specific niche. The key to Content Marketing is that the content MUST be created specifically to either attract new customers or retain the ones you already have. If it doesn't do this,then it is simply a 'waster' of time, energy and money. Today, the first thing anyone does when searching for more information about a person, company, product or service is to "Google" it. This concept is the reason why Content Marketing is so important; it's about getting your information out to the consumer whenever and wherever they look for it. In other words, be every place your consumer is, and today, most importantly, that's online.

TYPES OF CONTENT MARKETING

There are many types of Content Marketing, and while I sway toward online forms of Content Marketing, it is important to remember the off-line types as well.

Examples of online Content Marketing:

• Downloadable White Papers

• Downloadable Special Reports

• Ebooks

• Videos

• Podcasts

• Ezines

• Blogs

• Articles

• Press Releases

Examples of offline Content Marketing:

• Books

• Magazines

• Newsletters

• Sales letters

• Post cards

• Other Direct Mail Pieces

One thing to keep in mind when developing Content Marketing for your industry is that some types of Content Marketing may work better than others for your niche. So, be sure to test each type, and if you are still unsure, ask your audience their preference. You don't necessarily need to implement all of these strategies if they do not fit your particular business,but if you are looking to gain more customers and are not utilizing one or more of these strategies, then it might be something to look at.

DISTRIBUTION OF CONTENT MARKETING

As I stated before, *content is king on the Internet*; however, it is only as good as your marketing. You must put your content into the hands of your prospects and be where they are... This, quite frankly, may not be on your website. It doesn't matter where they find your information,what matters is that they find it, and that it is valuable enough that they then visit your website or, better yet, contact you directly.

SEO (search engine optimization) and Content Marketing go hand-in hand. SEO helps you improve your organic rankings in search engines. In other words, it is what allows you to come up in the search engine results when someone searches for keywords related to your productor service.

To properly promote your content and make sure it is in front of your searching prospects, you must understand (or hire someone who understands) SEO and the importance of <u>seeding all content you produce with keywords</u> – specifically, the correct keywords for your industry. If you're unsure of your keywords, Google has an excellent keyword tool that helps you find out just what your prospects are searching for, visit: https://adwords.google.com/select/KeywordToolExternal.

Once you know your keywords, here are some ways to distribute your online Content Marketing pieces:

- **Social Media Sites-** The biggest ones out there right now that we are currently using are http://www.Twitter.com, http://www.Facebook.com and http://www.Linkedin.com.

- **Social Bookmarking-** Social bookmarking allows you share your content online by publicly book marking your content. Think of it like bookmarking something in a magazine or book so it can easily be found later or shared with others. That's the idea behind social bookmarking, sharing useful content with others. The best tool we use is http://www.sociallist.net, which allows you to submit to approximately 50 bookmarking sites at one time including the biggest ones like http://www.digg.com, http://www.delicious.com, http://www.stumpleupon.com and http://www.reddit.com.

- **Article Syndication-** One of the biggest article-syndication sites is http://www.ezinearticles.com. Another top article-syndication site we use is http://www.submityourarticle.com. It's a paid source, but with only a few clicks it allows you to submit your articles to 12-15 additional article-syndication sites. We also use http://knol.google.com/k, http://www.hubpages.comand http://www.squidoo.com to syndicate articles.

- **Video Syndication-** The biggest video syndications site is http://www.youtube.com. However, we also like http:///www.tubemogul.com, which not only allows you to submit videos to YouTube but also allows you to submit to about 15 other video sites at the same time. A complete time saver if you think about all of the uploads you would have to do (and it's FREE!).

- **Press Release Syndication-** Two of the biggest online press release syndication sources we use on a regular basis (and they are both free) are: http://www.prlog.org and http://www.pitchengines.com.

- **Other Industry Related Blogs-** Find other blogs in your industry (or newspapers/magazines with columns in your industry) and offer to guest write a blog (or blog column) for them. You can develop a loyal following by providing great content to these additional blog sites. You can also comment on other blogs in your industry, and by commenting regularly and with good information you will see an increase in traffic to your site. Looking for a blog that you can guest blog on? Check out http://myblogguest.com.

MEASURING CONTENT MARKETING

Measuring Content Marketing can be a little tricky, as you are not always able to directly measure the value of someone "Googling" your name, company or keywords. What is the value of someone's confidence in you and your company by the information that they find? Not always easily measured, yet, VERY important. However, here are some

things that you can track to determine the affect your Content Marketing is having on your business. Think in terms of not direct profit numbers, but the effect that educating the consumer has on your website and your business.

- Repeat visitors
- Comments on your blog
- How long people stay on your website
- How many pages people view on your website
- Newsletter subscriptions
- Website downloads
- Referring sites (email, Social Bookmarking Sites, Social Media Sites)
- Gaining more "friends" on Twitter
- Gaining more "fans" or "friends" on Facebook

All of the above are signals that your Content Marketing strategies are working.

Although it can be tough to measure the power of someone "Googling" you and finding third-party verification of who you are and what you do, there are some ways that you can specifically measure your Content

Marketing Strategies, here are a couple of examples:

- Separate 800 numbers (check out http://www.yourroiguy.com)
- Individual URLs for different projects
- Make sure every web page has a call to action that you track conversions on

BENEFITS OF CONTENT MARKETING

The most important benefit about Content Marketing is that it allows you to compete with the "big dogs" in your industry. You may not be able to buy an ad for the Super Bowl, but with the Internet, distribution of content marketing has little or no cost. Here are some other benefits of Content Marketing:

- Generate more traffic to your website
- Build a loyal following
- Build a list from opt-ins on your website
- Increase brand awareness on the Internet
- Establish yourself (and your business) as the "go-to" expert in your niche

Key Things to Help With Content Marketing :

- Content Marketing can seem a bit overwhelming, so make an action plan ahead of time - at least six months in advance, of what you are going to distribute to potential and current clients and also how you will distribute the information.

- Old rule of thumb, seven impressions to create awareness of an ad – so, in theory, this means that each piece of your Content Marketing should be created in a series. This means create aseries of videos, a series of white papers, a series of blogs, etc.

- Content MUST be intrinsically important to your customer for it to play a vital role in your content marketing strategy. Don't just distribute content to distribute content, make sure it's valuable to your consumer or prospect.

- You MUST understand your customers and what is important to them - this includes any problems or frustrations they face. If you do not understand them, you cannot begin to deliver valuable relevant content.

- Content Marketing can be in conjunction with, or completely replace, traditional advertising.

- Great design adds value to Content Marketing by making it more appealing, accessible and easier to understand.

- Look both internally and externally for content - your employees may be your biggest asset when it comes to content marketing. What are they doing that you can re purpose into great content?

- Don't forget about direct mail as a part of content marketing,and the advantages that sending someone a magazine or postcard can have.

- Regardless of where your content ends up - the goal is to get your message out there. It ultimately doesn't matter if someone engages with your content on your website or someone else's, as long as it makes them take action.

- A good website with relevant and valuable content is the first step, but you MUST make it easy for them to buy and/or "raise their hand." Make sure your calls to action are on every page.

- *Good content can trump big dollars!*

IN SUMMARY

Remember, the entire principle of Content Marketing is that we have moved away from a sales position into an educational position. By sharing information vital to your niche, you become an authority and those in your target group will want to pursue a relationship with you. How do you do this? Educate the consumers by providing good, valuable and useful information, thus staying in the forefront of their minds and when they need your service.... ***THEY WILL THINK OF YOU!!!!***

About Lindsay

Lindsay Dicks helps her clients tell their stories in the online world. Being brought up around a family of marketers, but a product of Generation Y, Lindsay naturally gravitated to the new world of on-line marketing. Lindsay began freelance writing in 2000 and soon after launched her own PR firm that thrived by offering an in-your-face "Guaranteed PR" that was one of the first of its type in the nation.

Lindsay's new media career is centered on her philosophy that "people buy people." Her goal is to help her clients build a relationship with their prospects and customers. Once that relationship is built and they learn to trust them as the expert in their field, then they will do business with them. Lindsay also built a proprietary process that utilizes social media marketing, content marketing and search engine optimization to create online "buzz" for her clients that helps them to convey their business and personal story. Lindsay's clientele span the entire business map and range from doctors and small business owners to Inc 500 CEOs.

Lindsay is a graduate of the University of Florida. She is the CEO of CelebritySites™, an online marketing company specializing in social media and online personal branding. Lindsay is recognized as one of the top online marketing experts in the world and has co-authored more than 25 best-selling books alongside authors such as Brian Tracy, Jack Canfield (creator of the "Chicken Soup for the Soul" series), Dan Kennedy, Robert Allen, Dr. Ivan Misner (founder of BNI), Jay Conrad Levinson (author of the "Guerilla Marketing" series), Leigh Steinberg and many others, including the breakthrough hit *Celebrity Branding You!*

She was also selected as one of America's PremierExperts™ and has been quoted in *Newsweek, The Wall Street Journal, USA Today,* and *Inc.* magazine as well as featured on NBC, ABC, and CBS television affiliates speaking on social media, search engine optimization and making more money online. Lindsay was also recently brought on FOX 35 News as their Online Marketing Expert.

Lindsay, a national speaker, has shared the stage with some of the top speakers in the world, such as Brian Tracy, Lee Milteer, Ron LeGrand, Arielle

Ford, David Bullock, Brian Horn, Peter Shankman and many others. Lindsay was also a Producer on the Emmy-winning film, *Jacob's Turn*.

You can connect with Lindsay at:
Lindsay@CelebritySites.com
www.twitter.com/LindsayMDicks
www.facebook.com/LindsayDicks

CHAPTER 3

ALIGN YOUR DREAMS, GOALS, AND VALUES FOR LASTING SUCCESS

BY JW DICKS

In the many training sessions I have hosted over the years, I have noticed a great number of people have a difficult time with goal setting. They understand intellectually the value of setting goals, but they can't see how it applies to their own lives.

Maybe this sounds self-evident, but I'll say it anyway: Before you can set a goal, you have to understand what a goal is. Simply put, _a goal is a dream fixed to a certain time_. The dream is something you desire. The time element affixes it to your personal world and your reality. The dream is no longer simply floating in space; now it has a real "time meaning" attached to it, and it must be dealt with.

Second, the goal must relate to a personal value. Goals are the answer to the question, _"What is important to you in life?"_ Values are the answer to why you want to accomplish those goals. If you don't relate your goal to your values, that goal will remain as lost – floating in space – as it was before you attached it to the reality of time.

This is one reason why you can't simply adopt someone else's goals for your life. The chances that you'll share that person's deepest values

31

are incredibly small. Therefore, a goal that makes sense to another person isn't likely to make much sense to you.

It is also why it is foolish for parents to push their children onto a particular career path, or – worse – into accomplishing something that they had not been able to achieve for themselves. Why? Because the goal that is being set for the child is based on the *parents'* dream rather than the child's. Yes, you can help someone nurture his or her own dreams,but you can't dream for someone else. The most rewarding thing a parent can do for a child is help that child discover their own dreams and learn how to fulfill them.

SHAPE YOUR DREAMS

In order to reach a goal you set for yourself, you must first learn to define it specifically. If you are unsure of your objective, it will be easy for you to become distracted. For example, if you start only with the general desire to "make more money," you may achieve that goal – but chances are you won't keep the money. You'll soon discover that there is no end to the amount you can spend if you don't relate it to certain standards. The 2,500 square-foot house will become the 5,000 square-foot house. The"first new car" will evolve into the "first luxury car," which will evolve into the "top of the line new car traded in every two years."

Because you have no specific goal, you will be trapped on the 'up escalator'. You will spend more and more, because you think that the very acquisition of things will make you happy. Yes, you will find yourself in new, more luxurious surroundings – but instead of worrying about how you are going to make your $700 per-month house payment,you'll be worrying about how you will make the $4,000 per-month house payment.

You achieved your vague goal – *more money* – but somehow things got worse. The topic of worry (lack of money) has stayed the same, but now the practical burden you bear has become far heavier. You had a certain number of options to find replacement cash flow for the

$700 per-month payment on your smaller home. But now that your payments are $4,000 per-month, the options available to you for producing that much money are far fewer.

To stay off the up escalator – to avoid the "more money" treadmill – you need to decide what you do want, and in very precise terms. You need to *shape your dreams* by attaching them to time frames and specifics. At the same time, you need to make sure that the goals you set are aligned with your values.

Why? Because your values are the focal point of your internal happiness. If you set and achieve a goal that is in conflict with your values, not only will you be unhappy about having obtained that goal, but the result will have a negative influence on your desire to set and achieve other goals. Psychologically, you will begin to regard goal setting as an unhappy experience,even though that wasn't the problem in the first place. The real problem was that you didn't align the goals with your values.

I have some very good friends who worked for years to build a large company out of an idea they came up with together. They longed fort he day when they could buy a huge house on the water in a very exclusive area of our town. Because of their diligence and hard work, the company prospered, and they achieved their goal of purchasing their dream home. Unfortunately, the achievement of that goal didn't make them happy. Why not? Because that purchase separated them from their friends and their church, both of which – as it turned out – were things that they valued far more than that new house on the water.

And just to make things worse, they began to feel guilty about their newfound wealth. They worried that people might think they were showing off – even though that had never been their intent – and that people might become less friendly toward them. And in fact, their friends did begin to associate with them less frequently – in part because of their own feelings of jealousy and insecurity, and in part because their old friends now seemed different in their fancy new house. They seemed guarded and defensive rather than open and friendly.

While this couple came to understand the causes of what had happened, it didn't make them feel any better. The mistake they made was not in buying a big house on the water. (There's nothing inherently wrong with that goal.) The mistake they made was that they had defined and achieved a goal that didn't match their values. How do you keep your goals and values aligned?

I have summarized the process in a series of seven steps:

1. Create a list of goals and values.

2. Prioritize your goals.

3. Establish a plan to achieve your goals.

4. Take action on your goals.

5. Create success habits.

6. Rebalance your key objectives.

7. Enjoy, actualize, and repeat the process.

GOAL-SETTING STRATEGY NO. 1: CREATE A LIST OF GOALS AND VALUES

Values are what you believe about yourself. Goals, on the other hand, are targets that should capture those values and – once achieved – reinforce those values. In the case of my friends who became isolated, their goal was a hollow one, because it took them away from their fundamental values of friends and church. The goal was clearly at odds with their values. Without an alignment between values and goals, there will be no satisfaction. In fact, the only possible outcome is dissatisfaction.

Discovering your own values is one of the most important things you can do. And yet, very few people have ever even considered their values. Here is a short helpful exercise. Sit down in a quiet room and write down five personal values that you consider important. Don't think too hard about it – just start writing what comes into your mind. They will come to you. If you put down more than five, that's fine (you won't be graded!).

If you need help getting started, that's OK, too. Just glance at this list of values shared by many people. Remember that while lists of values may overlap (in other words, you may use the same words as someone else), the order of the words and the weight you place upon them make the lists very different.

A close relationship with your mate

A good relationship with your family

A meaning of life

A relationship with God

Being highly regarded

Control of your destiny

Fame

Friendships

Giving to others

Good health

Happiness

Influence

Living to old age

Peace of mind

Possessions

Power

Purpose to work

Respect

Retirement

Security

Sense of accomplishment

Travel

Wealth

YOUR VALUE LIST :

1. _____

2. _____

3. _____

4. _____

5. _____

Now that you have made your list, rank your values from more important to less important (even though every value on this list is important).

Look at the result. Did you get it right? Are you happy with this summary of your values? If so, congratulations, because coming up with this list may be the most important thing you will ever do. Why? *Because it is truly your road map to happiness.*

Here's why. Let's assume that your number one value is a close relationship with God, and your number two value is a close relationship with your family. And let's also assume that at the present time, you are pursuing a career that pays well and earns you lots of kudos and recognition but requires you to spend a great deal of time away from your family.

Well, if that job doesn't somehow help you to develop a closer relationship with God, you are likely to be one miserable human being – and chances are, you won't even know why. Most likely, you are working hard, banking a lot of money, and feeling mostly empty inside. Your values are your essence. If you hope to achieve a happy life, you have to live a life and aspire to a future that captures and expresses those values.

Assume for a moment that a certain individual (let's call her Jane) has the following values:

1. A close relationship with God

2. A close relationship with family

3. Peace of mind

4. Security

5. Good health

Conspicuously absent from Jane's list is anything about "making lots of money." True, you could make the case that goals 3 through 5 presuppose financial security. But the point is, "making money" didn't make Jane's list.

Can you see the importance of this discovery? If Jane spends all of her time trying to become a millionaire, she is almost certain to be a very unhappy millionaire (if, indeed, she ever gets there). For Jane to be successfulin her own eyes, her goals must be aligned with her values. Tosharpen the point, let's consider the following question: Which of thefollowing goals, if achieved, would make Jane happier?

1. Making $1 million.

2. Setting up a faith-based charitable foundation with an endowment of $1 million.

See the difference? Putting $1 million in the bank would probably make Jane feel OK, up to a point. But wouldn't endowing a faith-based charitable foundation do a lot more to make Jane feel satisfied with her life?

Let's take this illustration a step further. What if you changed the second goal to read: "Setting up a faith-based charitable foundation with an endowment of $1 million, in which all of my family members would work together." Wow! Do you see what that would mean to Jane? The betters he understands her values, the more likely it is that she can set the right goals, give herself a life's mission, and live her life with passion.

So here's our next exercise, which builds directly on the last one, as well as on Jane's example. Take a few minutes to review the values you've written down and ranked. Now write down five goals that, if achieved, would capture and reinforce those values.

LIST GOALS

1. _____

2. _____

3. _____

4. _____

5. _____

GOAL-SETTING STRATEGY NO. 2: PRIORITIZE YOUR GOALS

Now that you have established a list of goals, rank them. Renumber them as you did your values list, lining them up in their order of importance to you. And although we don't want to complicate the assignment too much, we encourage you to think about making two such lists: one ranked in order of importance, and the second ranked in order of urgency. Which goal is of the greatest enduring importance to you, and which do you want (or need) to accomplish first?

For example, if one of your goals is to build a $2 million retirement nest egg and another is to put your kids through college five years from now, it doesn't make a great deal of sense to concentrate on your retirement plan when you have a much more urgent need – unless, of course, the retirement plan is of far greater importance to you. If the goals are of equal importance, then urgency takes over, and your priority quickly becomes the tuition bills.

GOAL-SETTING STRATEGY NO. 3:
ESTABLISH A PLAN TO ACHIEVE YOUR GOALS

You have your goal. It is your top priority. Now, what are you going to do about it?

When my children were younger we went on trips by car, I would call the American Automobile Association – "Triple A"— and ask them to do a trip plan. In a couple of weeks, AAA would send back a nice, bound series of maps that told us the best way to get to our destinations. (Now, of course, you can do it all online.) If there was construction along the way, AAA would either suggest detours or carefully mark the construction area and advise us that there was a bumpy road ahead.

Wouldn't it be nice if life were like that? You could set your goal, call up AAA, and get a plan laid out for you. Unfortunately, life isn't quite that easy. But with the help of the simple concepts you can learn how to do the plan yourself. The key to reaching any financial goal is to have a plan. Surprisingly, it's not so important that you pick the perfect road or the perfect investment system. Instead, the important thing is to pick a specific plan and stick with it until you reach your destination.

How do you create a plan to achieve your goals? The same way that you create a plan for a trip. You write down the moves that you need to make, step by step, to get to your destination. Just as you follow a map from AAA to get to a geographic destination, you follow a specific plan to get to a goal destination.

GOAL-SETTING STRATEGY NO. 4:
TAKE ACTION ON YOUR GOALS

My father always said, "A turtle never gets anywhere unless he sticks his neck out." He was right. Ultimately, we have to take action. Otherwise,all our values, goals, and plans aren't worth the paper we put them on.

But taking action proves difficult for a lot of people, because they are filled with anxieties and insecurities. Did I put down the right goal? Is my plan a good one? These doubts paralyze the worrier, just like a deer caught in headlights.

Nevertheless, you must take action on the plan you create. Think of it as something like scaling a cliff. If you had to climb a cliff for the first time, how would you do it? You'd start out slow and easy. You'd pace yourself, going up foot by vertical foot. You don't have to break any speed record or take any unnecessary risks. Well, it's the same with acting on a goal plan. You don't have to reach your goal overnight. Success is an endurance event – a marathon rather than a sprint. Take off slowly, build to a comfortable pace, and stride to the finish.

How do you get started? It's easy. Take a look at your goals list. Pick the one goal on your list that seems the easiest to accomplish and also has near-term importance. Let's say that you wrote down, "Make $10,000 more this year." That's a good goal. It's near-term, and it's specific. So let's use it to take action. Below your goal, create a plan to achieve the goal by listing the specific action steps you'll take to get there:

Goal:- Make $10,000 more this year

Plan:- Increase salary by $3,000

Action Step 1: Ask for a raise.

- Create a list of reasons I deserve a raise.
- Make an appointment with my boss.

<u>Action Step 2:</u> Start a small business.

• Research businesses of interest.

• Pick a business in 60 days.

• Start the business in 90 days.

If you are like a lot of people who have never properly learned the techniques of goal setting, this method is likely to come as a pleasant surprise. For the first time, not only do you see your goal, but you see specific action steps that you can take to achieve it.

While the goal may seem difficult, the action steps to achieve the goal are often much easier. You will discover that taking each step puts you closer and closer to your goal, which in turn makes the goal appear easier and more attainable the closer you get to it.

GOAL-SETTING STRATEGY NO. 5:
CREATE SUCCESS HABITS

Sometimes, with the best of intentions, parents do their children a disservice. One example of such a disservice is continuously linking the words habit and bad. For example:

Quit biting your nails. It's a bad habit.

Stop smoking. It's a bad habit.

Don't drink so much. It's a bad habit.

Have you ever heard anyone praised for developing a good habit? Not often, and yet, good habits are critically important. The tennis star's consistent stroke, which leads to victories on the court, is the result of a good habit. The student who studies consistently and makes top grades has developed good study habits. In fact, any repetitive pattern that brings success deserves to be recognized and applauded, and should be built intone's system of goals: I will continue this action until it becomes a habit.

Vital habits can be developed to help you maintain your success. For example, in investing, diversifying your portfolio, setting limits on losses, resisting the temptation to get greedy – all are proven goal rules that build both protection and consistency into your goal plan. If you take the time and effort to transform these goals into habits, you will profit substantially from the improved performance of your portfolio and the added protection they give you.

GOAL-SETTING STRATEGY NO 6:
REBALANCE YOUR KEY OBJECTIVES

I hope that, by now, you have been impressed on the importance of values and goals when it comes to your success. You should also understand that while some values may be consistent throughout your life, others may change. When they do, both your goals and your plans to reach those goals need to re-evaluated and rebalanced, in order to get your new value/goal structure into alignment. If you don't rebalance,it will be like deciding to stay on the road to New York after you've decided to go to San Francisco instead. Yes, you're still moving along a path, but you're sure to arrive at the wrong place.

To help you spot these changes as they occur in your life, I suggest that you set a particular time each year to rebalance your objectives. I have found the two weeks after Christmas to be a perfect time for this activity. Business always slows down during that time of year, and the decrease in activity gives you an opportunity to reflect.

Note the consistency in this approach. By consistently rebalancing your objectives at the same time each year, you have made this activity into a habit. While that time might not be good for you, pick one that is, rebalance your objectives, and (if necessary) refocus your life.

GOAL-SETTING STRATEGY NO. 7:
ENJOY, ACTUALIZE, AND REPEAT THE PROCESS

If you incorporate the six strategies, or steps, just outlined into your life, you will find a new sense of gratification and enjoyment. Now that your life is in alignment with who you are, you should begin to feel that you are headed in the right direction – much like the driver with the AAA road maps. Take the time to enjoy this newfound sense of satisfaction.

At the same time, be prepared for that sense of satisfaction to ebb and even disappear. Just as the wheels on your car lose their alignment over time (and far more quickly if you hit a curb!), our lives also get "out of alignment" because of life's curbs. It is just a part of human nature: We get caught up in all sorts of things that we never intended to get caught up in.

What's important, though, is simply to understand that we must (1) enjoy things when they go well, (2) understand that misalignment will happen, and (3) get realigned when we hit that curb (or when life's twists and turns gradually lead to misalignment).

By repeating this process, you will enjoy your life more and continually refocus yourself on the things that are truly important to you. **Once you are properly focused, it is easier to let go of those miscues that don't fit into your grand plan.**

About JW

JW Dicks, Esq., is America's foremost authority on using personal branding for business development. He has created some of the most successful brand and marketing campaigns for business and professional clients to make them the credible celebrity experts in their field and build multi-million dollar businesses using their recognized status.

JW Dicks has started, bought, built, and sold a large number of businesses over his 39-year career and developed a loyal international following as a business attorney, author, speaker, consultant, and business experts' coach. He not only practices what he preaches by using his strategies to build his own businesses, he also applies those same concepts to help clients grow their business or professional practice the ways he does.

JW has been extensively quoted in such national media as *USA Today,* the *Wall Street Journal, Newsweek, Inc.*, Forbes.com, CNBC.com, and *Fortune Small Business.* His television appearances include ABC, NBC, CBS and FOX affiliate stations around the country. He is the resident branding expert for *Fast Company*'s internationally syndicated blog and is the publisher of *Celebrity Expert Insider*, a monthly newsletter targeting business and brand-building strategies.

JW has written over 22 books, including numerous best-sellers, and has been inducted into the National Academy of Best-Selling Authors. JW is married to Linda, his wife of 39 years, and they have two daughters, two granddaughters and two Yorkies. JW is a 6th generation Floridian and splits his time between his home in Orlando and beach house on the Florida west coast.

CHAPTER 4

EARNING POTENTIAL IS YOUR MOST VALUABLE ASSET

BY BRIAN TRACY

What you are about to learn changed my life and it will change yours as well, in a positive way.

When I first heard the question, "What is your most valuable asset?", I immediately thought of my car, my furniture, my house, my investments and money in the bank. But these are not your most valuable financial assets. Your most valuable asset is your "earning ability." It is your ability to earn money each day, week, month and year. It is your ability to enter into a competitive market place and use your acquired and accumulated talent, skills, intelligence and ability to achieve results for which people will pay you 'good money'.

You could lose your house, your car, your job, and all your money, ending up penniless on the street. But, as long as you have maintained your earning ability and were able to re-enter the marketplace, you could pump tens of thousands of dollars back into your life. You could make all back, and more besides.

Because of our rapidly changing economy, and the continuing obsolescence of knowledge and skills, your earning ability can be either an"appreciating asset" or a "depreciating asset". If your earning ability is an "appreciating asset," you are becoming increasingly valuable every week, month and year. You are continually upgrading your existing skills and adding new knowledge and skills. These will enable you to get even better results for which people will pay you even more money.

For most people who are not aware of the importance of their earning ability, they have a "depreciating asset." It is continually losing value year by year, because the individual is not getting better and better at what he does. Even worse, most people are getting worse in the essentials kills required by their jobs. They are progressively worth less and less.

Pat Riley, the basketball coach, said, *"If you're not getting better, you're getting worse."* No one stays in the same place in a time of rapid change.

Peter Drucker said, *"The only skill that will be of lasting value in the 21st century will be the skill of learning new skills. All other skills will become obsolete with the passing of time."*

YOUR MOST PRECIOUS RESOURCE

Here is another question: What is your most precious resource? It is not something tangible or material. Your most precious resource is actually your "time." Your time represents your life itself. Your life is made up of the minutes and hours of each day. Once time has passed,it can never be retrieved. Once a minute or an hour has gone by, that amount of your life has passed as well.

One more question: *What is your very best investment?*

Answer: The very best investment you can make is to invest your time into increasing your earning ability. There is nothing that will improve the quality of your life, boost your income, and enable you to enjoy abetter lifestyle than by "getting better" at what you do today to earn your income.

You have heard about the 80/20 Rule. This rule, the "Pareto Principle," says that 20% of your activities will account for 80% of your results, and 20% of the things that you do in your work will account for 80% of your income.

This rule also says that the top 20% of people in any society earn and control 80% of the wealth. The bottom 80% of money earners have to struggle and get by on whatever is left over by those in the top 20%.

Why does this happen? Why do some people earn several times the income of others? As it happens, everyone starts off roughly at the same point. We have roughly the same education, intelligence and opportunity. Like a marathon, we all line up on the starting line and then the gun goes off. In the months and years ahead, some people move to the front, the bulk stay in the middle, and many people fall to the back, not even completing the race until everyone has gone home.

INCOME GAP VERSUS SKILLS GAP

There is a good deal of talk today about the "income gap" in our society. But Gary Becker, the 1993 Nobel Price winning economist, has pointed out that we do not have an "income gap" as much as we have a "skills gap."

The people in the top 20% are simply those who have learned the essential skills that they need to achieve a high level of earning ability. The people in the bottom 80% are those who, having had the same opportunity, failed to develop those skills.

Many people have gone from rags to riches by realizing this critical fact, and then dedicating themselves to become very good at what they do. You must do the same.

Every person who is serious about their future, especially their financial future, should commit to being in the top 10% of their field. What we have found is that anything less than a commitment to excellence condemns a person to being mediocre.

It seems as if there is a "default setting" on human performance. If you don't decide to become the best, you simply become average. Nobody sets off in life to be "average" or below. But by failing to dedicate yourself totally, especially in the formative years of your career, and by failing not to becoming absolutely excellent at what you do, you default into the bottom 80%, where you worry about money all your life.

In the 21st Century, you are a "knowledge worker." You do not work with your physical body, making and moving things. You work with your mind, applying your intelligence and personality to your world to make a valuable contribution that others will pay you for. The key to becoming an effective knowledge worker is for you to continually upgrade your knowledge and skills in the work that you have chosen to do.

KEY RESULT AREAS

In each job, there seems to be about five to seven *Key Result Areas* that account for performance, effectiveness and results in that job. You may perform dozens of small tasks in the course of a day or a week, but there are seldom more than five to seven key tasks that determine your success or failure.

For example, in Management, the seven *Key Result Areas* are:- 1) Planning; 2) Organizing; 3) Staffing; 4) Delegating; 5) Supervising; 6) Measuring; and 7) Reporting. Your success as a manager can largely be determined by how well you do your job and perform these functions in each area.

In Selling, for example, the seven *Key Result Areas* are:- 1) Prospecting and getting appointments; 2) Establishing rapport and trust; 3) Identifying customer needs accurately; 4) Presenting your products persuasively; 5) Answering customer objections and concerns; 6) Closing the sale and getting the customer to take action; and 7) Getting resales and referrals from satisfied customers.

In summary, this is what we have discovered: Your weakest key skill in your field determines the 'height' of your income and your success.

Your weakest essential skill is what holds you back from performing at your very best in all of the other areas. By identifying your weakest skill, and then becoming excellent in that area, you can often surge ahead rapidly in your career and move up into the top 10%.

YOUR MOST IMPORTANT SKILL

How do you determine the skill that can help you the most? You ask this question: "What one skill, if I was absolutely excellent at, would help me the most to double my income?"

If you are not sure about your answer to this question, you must find out as quickly as possible. Ask your boss. Ask your coworkers. Ask your friends. Ask your customers. *You must know the answer to this question or you cannot move ahead in your career.* It is impossible for you to get into the top 10% in your field unless you know with great clarity which skill, or lack of skill, is holding you back.

Once you have determined the one skill that can help you the most, write it down as a goal using these words: "I am absolutely excellent at this particular skill by (such and such a date)."

Then, make a list of everything you could do to develop this skill. Organize the list by sequence and priority. What do you need to do before you do something else? What is more important and what is less important? A list of activities, organized by sequence and priorities, becomes a plan. With a goal and a plan, you will start to make more progress in your life than you can imagine today.

The next step is for you to take action immediately on your new goal-that of becoming excellent in an area where you are still weak. Then, to complete your success, you must do something every single day that makes you a little bit better. Read a little bit in your field. Listen to audio programs in your car. Attend seminars and courses. And most of all, practice, practice, practice until you finally reach the top.

JOIN THE TOP 10%

When I first learned that I would have to be in the top 10% in my field in order to enjoy the highest possible income, I immediately felt discouraged and disappointed. I had never been good at anything before. I had been kicked out of high school in the 12th grade and had worked at laboring jobs for several years. When I got into sales, I knocked on hundreds of doors, cold-calling, and made almost no sales at all.

Now, a top sales professional was telling me that I would have to be in the top 10% to really enjoy all the riches and rewards of the selling profession. Then I learned something that changed my life. I learned that everyone who is in the top 10% started in the bottom 10%. Everyone who is doing well was once doing poorly. Everyone who is at the top of your field today was at one time not even in your field, and did not even know that your field existed.

Here is a great discovery:

All business skills are learnable. All sales skills are learnable. All management skills are learnable. All business building and entrepreneurial skills are learnable. All success-skills and money-making skills are learnable.

Everyone who is good at them today was at one time poor in every area. But they made a decision, set a goal, made a plan, and worked on it, over and over again, until they mastered the skill. And what hundreds of thousands and millions of other people have done, you can do as well.

NO ONE IS SMARTER THAN YOU

Remember, no one is smarter than you and no one is better than you. If someone is doing better than you today, it simply means that they have learned the essential skills they needed before you have. And anything anyone else has done, you can do as well.

When you follow this formula, concentrating on your most important and desirable skills, disciplining yourself to persist until you have mastered those skills, you will open up your whole life. You will put your career onto the fast track. You will increase your earning ability rapidly.

As you get better and better at a key skill, your self-esteem will increase. Your self-image will improve. You will like and respect yourself more, and you will be liked and respected more by the people around you. You will feel a tremendous sense of personal power and pride as you get better and better at what you do.

Sooner or later, in a month, six months, or a year, you will have mastered that key skill. Then what do you do? You repeat the process with the next one!

Once again, you ask, *"Now, what one skill will help me the most to double my income?"*

You write it down, make a plan, and work on it every day. <u>You turn yourself into a do-it-to-yourself project.</u>

FAST TRACK TO SUCCESS

Thousands of chief executive officers of large and small companies have been asked, "What qualities would most mark a person for rapid promotion in your company?"

Fully 85% of them give the same answer. They say: "The most valuablepeople in my company are those who set priorities, work on their mostimportant tasks, and get the job done quickly and well."

As you develop new skills, increasing (a) your earning ability, and (b) your levels of knowledge and skills, you must then apply what you know to getting important jobs done quickly.

<u>There is nothing that will cause you to stand out in your field more than by developing a reputation as a hard worker who does things quickly and well.</u>

In a short period of time, you will become the 'go-to' person in your company. When your boss, or other key people, want or need something done quickly, they will come to you. Along with these additional responsibilities will come additional authority, opportunity and increased income. *Your goal should be to become one of the most effective, most competent, most respected, and highest paid people in your business.*

The good news is that there are no limits to what you can accomplish, and how far you can go, when you dedicate your working life to continually increasing your earning ability. You will soon become one of the highest paid people in your field.

About Brian

Brian Tracy is Chairman and CEO of Brian Tracy International, a company specializing in the training and development of individuals and organizations. Brian's goal is to help people achieve their personal and business goals faster and easier than they ever imagined.

Brian Tracy has consulted for more than 1,000 companies and addressed more than 5,000,000 people in 5,000 talks and seminars throughout the US, Canada and 55 other countries worldwide. As a Keynote speaker and seminar leader, he addresses more than 250,000 people each year.

For more information on Brian Tracy programs, go to: www.briantracy.com

CHAPTER 5

EMPLOYERS BEWARE: FIVE LESSONS TO PROTECT YOUR WEALTH!

BY CLAUDIA BODUEL

Let's begin with a story.... this is a true story of how one employer decided to change what was his career. Instead of building beautiful kitchens, he involuntarily became an insurer.

This is how he did it:

Once upon a time there was this regular non-management employee in his early 50's, who had been with his employer for more than 20 years when he was dismissed without cause. The employer gave him the equivalent of nearly 32 weeks pay in lieu of notice. He also provided the employee with of 8 weeks' worth of benefits (including long term disability coverage). The former employee became seriously ill after a period of time, but still during the 32-week period. Not being unable to find suitable alternative work due to the fact that he was now disabled, the fellow turned to the legal system for help. The result was that the employer was found responsible for this former employee's disability benefits as if they were the insurer. This cost the employer just under $200,000 plus court costs and legal fees! And this amount would have been much higher if the worker had been younger. The employer was just lucky!

Welcome to the big leagues! Congratulations! You are an employer. This means, of course, that you have employees.... those other human beings who not only help you achieve your success, but also have expectations of success in return. This reciprocity takes many forms: a pay-cheque that clears regularly, vacation entitlements, opportunities for advancement, employee benefit coverage (above and beyond the government programs) and fair treatment.

By virtue of the fact that these human beings have entered into an employment contract, they have expectations, which in Canada, are protected by Employment Standards (minimum), Human Rights, and pay equity legislation. These rights are also protected by our Canadian courts in developing case law.

Considering our dismissed worker and his former employer's woes, why would you consider entering into employee benefits? Do you really just need another expense?

My name is Claudia Boduel, owner of Focused Benefit Solutions, Inc. I have been working in employee benefits in Canada for almost 30 years. The stories I could tell you! Well, actually, most people are not overly enthusiastic to speak about insurance. Or listen to it either, not unless it is to bash the big, bad, old insurance companies for not paying a claim. Or unless there is a copious amount of wine flowing! So thank you for reading this far. Most of my working career, I spent on the insurance company side, becoming a consultant in 2003. My role at the various insurance companies with which I worked, was to put employee benefit programs into place with client companies, when brokers or consultants awarded my employer the business. It was a real struggle to see how poorly most programs were handled, because their true protection power was either not understood, or not appreciated. The value of this sort of plan is truly that it protects the EMPLOYER while at the same time providing for the employees in times of hardship.

The BEST way to protect your good name, and wealth, is to recognize that the rules of engagement with your employees do not change whether you have an insured policy of some sort or not....just the dollar value you will pay out of cash flow changes....and premiums for properly set-up programs are the least expensive dollars you will ever spend.

Lesson 1: Insurance is cheaper than paying the full amount out of cash flow.

Back to our builder of beautiful Kitchens.... the most likely reasons that the offer of benefits was not extended beyond the first 8 weeks were:

1. Insurers will not grant benefits beyond the statutory requirement without some heavy duty negotiating!

2. Neither the employer, or his broker were aware that terminating benefits after 8 weeks was a dangerous move, or

3. The benefits consultant was not involved in the severance planning.

Lesson 2: The insurance company is not your alley, a competent insurance broker is! And with my years as an insurance company rep, I saw the value of a competent advisor. I also saw the damage the incompetent advisors caused!

What makes a consultant/broker/agent competent?

- It is not length of time in the insurance business because some people repeat their first year of work experience over and over again for 30 years! They have survived in the insurance business, but have not gained any useful knowledge. (They wouldn't know, for example, that our kitchen builder was left exposed to a hefty judgment, until it bit the client in the wallet).

- It is not their swanky office address.

- Is it the size of their organization? Perhaps.... If they have hired competent staff, and provide a proven method for identifying and solving your issues.

A competent consultant :

(1) has industry qualifications specific to employee benefits.

(2) Is highly regarded by insurers and peers (speaks to his/her negotiation equity).

(3) Has processes and programs in place to make a meaningful contribution to your trusted advisor team.

(4) Outlines service standards to which you both agree, and to which his/her team is held accountable.

(5) Will identify the risk issues you are unaware of, and has suggestions for reducing their impact on your bottom line.

(6) Seeks to understand your vision for your business, your vision for your employees and provides strategies/programs to assist in achieving these objectives. Is clear about their value proposition, and is transparent about their consulting fee.

(7) Can provide client testimonials that go beyond "yes, he/she is a great golfer! ...And a really, really, nice person!" Aw shucks!

Lesson 3: Find a competent consultant and be prepared to change consultants if your current advisor is found lacking. (By the way, all brokers, agents or consultants are compensated for the work they do, most often by commissions imbedded in the rates you pay. You have hired them, either by choice or by default.)

The taxman and his employer, our government, have their hands in our pockets all the time. After all, government programs and all government revenue are achieved either through taxation or a reduction of services provided. As an employer there is a 'double whammy" for both of these burdens of cost shifting to happen to you. Here's why:

In Canada, we have a safety net of government-supported health services as outlined in the Canada Health Act. Each province is responsible to manage their program as overseen by the Federal Government. The Federal government gives transfer payments to the

Provinces with which to manage the Provincial health services. These services include all hospital services such as surgery, all doctors' fees, medical testing, special-needs individuals, mental health initiatives... the list is extensive and the need is growing, especially with our aging population. Guess what? The government is finding it difficult to provide all the services it is supposed to be providing, those services Canadians assume the government is providing, those very services Canadians EXPECT to have provided! And so, they quietly, stealthily, have and continue to shift the burden of the expenses to private employer-sponsored plans! Your biggest financial risk comes from 'defined benefit' plans with few, if any limitations, which are often underfunded and misunderstood.

Lesson 4: Protect yourself against government off loading. The question you should ask yourself is this: If the government can't afford to provide these benefits, why would I?

All well and good! Still not sure you want anything to do with insurance for your employees? How about a program, which if followed, will allow you to safeguard your company against having to keep on payroll an employee you are not permitted to terminate, even while he/she is not actively at work?

And the beauty of this program is that it is normally funded by the employees! Doesn't that sound cost effective?

Employee benefits are important! In a recent benefits survey, the conclusions drawn stated that even though benefits were not the front and centre for attracting talent, benefits are the price of entry. In other words, you need a decent plan just to "play" -- to be in the game of getting those team members you need.

To have benefits or not to have benefits? What are the advantages for an employer?

First, the advantages of not having a plan:

   (1) No monthly premium of which the employer must fund to a minimum of half the cost.

(2) No concern with the customary annual cost increases.

(3) Could handle employee requirements on a one-off exception basis.

(4) Makes employees self-sufficient. (Learn to swim with the sharks!)

Disadvantages of not having a plan:

(1) Any exceptions you make for one employee, you must be prepared to make for others in similar circumstances, or run the risk of being accused of discriminatory practices. And without a plan, you are paying for everything out of cash flow.

(2) If employees are looking for a formal program, not having one makes the business look less successful.

(3) Any accommodation you as the employer make for an employee, you make without the aid of expert help. Further, as an employer you are not permitted to ask certain questions of an employee due to our Privacy legislation, so you run the risk of paying for benefits out of cash flow which are:

(i) not legitimate as permitted by the Income Tax Act , and

(ii) herefore not an eligible business expense.

Advantages to the employer of having an employee benefit plan:

(1) Speaks to the success of your business.

(2) Sets out the cost, and locks it in for a period of time.

(3) Sets out the coverage, both in terms of the scope and the limitations for all.

(4) Protects the employer against discriminatory practices.

(5) Hires competent claims adjudicators to make sure that all claims processed are permissible.

(6) Protects the employer from breaching the privacy act.

(7) Lets the adjudicator decline claims when necessary, therefore they are the "bad" guys, you are not!

(8) Outsources the absence management program to a third party who has the medical expertise.

(9) Is the least expensive way to expand the competency of your human resources.

So, one more time – back to our builder of beautiful kitchens and his disabled former employee...the cost of that mistake was well over $200,000. (This was the amount of the award to the employee, plus legal fees and court costs.)

The questions you might ask are:

1) Just how likely is this to happen anyway?

2) What is the exposure, or risk to me, the employer?

3) How else could this have been handled?

4) Is there a better way?

Here are the answers:

(1) Disability risk is very high. Statistics tells us that 1 in 3 of us will be disabled before age 65, and the average duration of the disability will be in excess of 3 years.[1]

(2) The exposure is 100%.

(3) This could have been handled with insurance! (Have you not been paying attention?)

(4) The premiums for the specialized insurance would have cost about $4,000.00 (give or take a few hundred dollars). This means the savings would have been a mere $196,000.00.

Lesson 5: Insurance is cheaper than paying the full amount out of cash flow.

Here is one concept you should really wrap your mind around: If you have a benefit consultant, or are entertaining an alternative bid, because you really want the same program you have now, only cheaper, how much money can you save if your tendering process is *exceedingly* successful? If courts become involved, the dollars become large.

We can worry and fuss about pennies, or we can protect ourselves against big losses. Program degradation can occur over time when the focus is taken off the real purpose of the program while attempting to drive the cost to below a reasonable level. Something's gotta give, and it is usually quality. And just to be clear, I am not saying that budgets and costs are not important. It is a given that the premium must be reasonable and responsible. My point is that if cost reduction is the sole focus, you are heading for trouble.

BONUS!

Lesson 6: Proper risk management of the employer-employee relationship, coupled with properly structured insurance programs, will reduce the number and size of potential unfunded liabilities and will offer protection for the bottom line value of the business. That is why an employee benefits program is really and truly an equity protection plan.

And Lesson 6 applies to all employers – whether or not you have a formal employee benefits program. If you have employees, you have exposure! Please make very sure your advisor is a competent consultant, and not just an order taker.

[N.B. Claudia Boduel is licensed to give insurance advice in Ontario, Alberta and British Columbia.]

---

1. Canada Life Insurance Co. provided statistic, based on the 1985 Commissioners Disability Table A 92 CIA Mortality table, blended 50/50 male/female

About Claudia

In 1985, Claudia Boduel found herself in the insurance business quite by accident. Her idea was to start in sales at a Canadian company, and then move into management, on her way up the corporate ladder. However, once she settled in to working with business owners and their employees, she found that empowering people to secure their financial futures was her passion. She saw first-hand how insurance done right, protects income and preserves equity.

While working for various insurance companies across Canada as a group account executive, Claudia became increasingly alarmed at the skill level of agents who believed themselves competent to 'do-it-all' themselves. Often, they structured programs poorly, leaving the company underinsured and 'underwhelmed' with their programs.

Claudia's newest venture, Focused Benefit Solutions Inc., is built on her philosophy that when clients hire professionals, they not only expect but also deserve competency, integrity, and expert advice. She interviews clients as much as they interview her, to see if working together is a good fit for both. Claudia has developed a process which not only works to align the client-company's vision for their employees with the actual insurance program, but her company also provides ancillary programs to assist employers in setting corporate policies, and communicating the program fully to end-users to avoid surprises.

Claudia surrounds herself with professionals in complimentary fields such as human resources, employment law, business succession planning, executive search experts and financial planners, to be able to make introductions and to build the client's team of trusted advisors.

Claudia is a graduate of York University and has achieved Fellow Status with her Certified Employee Benefits Specialist designation from Dalhousie University. She worked for five major insurance companies in both Toronto and Vancouver over 18 years before partnering with a financial planner in 2003 to build a group benefits consulting firm in the Vancouver area. In 2012, Claudia created Focused Benefit Solutions Inc. in order to make the consulting work she had always dreamed of a reality. Claudia is married to Oliver, who is her life partner and biggest supporter in her business ventures. Oliver and Claudia have 2 successful adult daughters, who live near-by.

To get further info on Claudia, finding a competent broker or structuring a plan for maximum effectiveness, visit: www.focusedbenefitsolutions.com, or send an email.

(N.B. Claudia Boduel is licensed to give insurance advice in Ontario, Alberta and British Columbia.)

CHAPTER 6

LIVING IN VICTORY: THROUGH THE POWER OF FORGIVENESS

BY JENNIFER LEE

I remember a glimpse of happiness – a period of innocence where life was peaceful and joyful; where children played with one another and life was simple and filled with love, laughter and trust. Doors in our village were seldom locked and neighbors visited us unannounced to share a meal, or simply to get together and care for one another - like an extended family. We are not Cambodian, but Chinese-Teochewnese. My family was prominent and successful business owners importing and exporting goods in China, Laos, Cambodia, and Vietnam.

Cambodia is a country with near-perfect farming conditions. I remember our two-story colonial style home, overlooking a river with a wide variety of exotic fruit trees that grew alongside our home. We could easily pick fruit from our balcony. We would pick coconuts, pomegranates, bananas, mangoes or papayas, and then sell them from our front yard – always the entrepreneurs.

These are some of my wonderful memories of the more carefree days of my early childhood living in Cambodia.

Suddenly, my whole world turned upside down and everything I enjoyed came to an abrupt end. In April of 1975, the Khmer Rouge

Regime and Pol Pot installed an extremist doctrine of communism from the Soviet Union and the People's Republic of China designed to create equality overnight. They took control of the government by a coup d'état and killed university professors, business owners, religious leaders, and foreign nationals. Eventually, the Cambodian people were not willing to submit to their rule.

America was invading Cambodia and bombing our cities, they told us. Fear and chaos filled the air. Victim's cries and wailings were heard everywhere. Families stripped of their possessions were forced to migrate to the countryside. Many were forced to walk through landmines to their deaths. As we walked, we saw endless dead bodies – decomposed and swollen. We saw countless bodies floating down the Mekong River.

These were the Killing Fields, and I am a Khmer Rouge genocide survivor and this is my story.

At the age of seven, I was forcefully removed from my family. My parents, sisters and brother were separated into different concentration camps. Everything had been taken from us at gunpoint. We walked along the Mekong River and I was placed into a slave camp with other children. We were to work in the rice-field trenches in mud and scorching heat twelve hours a day every day. Soldiers shot children in front of the others to make an example of what happens for disobedience.

One day my family was gathered from the other camps. I recount the loud wailing on this dreadful night. We had a few hours to say good-bye to our dad. He was taken away to an execution camp. That was and still is the saddest day of my life. Besides my dad, I lost three siblings. This brutality went on for 4 years. During this period nearly 3 million people died.

In January 1979, the Viet Cong invaded Cambodia and the Khmer Rouge regime dissolved. We returned to our villages to look for our families. When I was reunited with my family, I could hardly recognize them. We all looked like poster children you may have seen in an ad to feed the poor.

Empty handed and without any money, my mom found a way to get us to Vietnam to live with our relatives. My mom dreamt of bringing her children to America. She gathered enough money to pay a guide to take us to the refugee camp in Thailand through Cambodia. Traveling on foot day and night we faced dangerous paths. Khmer Rouge soldiers continued to gun down civilians. We treaded through landmines and tip toed past swollen dead bodies.

We finally arrived at the refugee camp. A tent was used to house the refugees. There were no curtains. Privacy did not exist. It was in these conditions where we hoped to get sponsorship from the United Nations or a church organization. In the refugee camp we faced "night terror" frequently. I can recall the nights our family was taken out and forced to our knees at gunpoint. Soldiers demanded money and gold. Mom would spend hours begging for our lives.

The happiest day of our lives finally arrived. We got sponsorship from a church organization. We soon boarded a plane for America. We landed in Atlanta, Georgia in the winter of 1982 along with five other refugee families. Mom recalled she had only $50 dollars to feed her children.

Church people came to visit, provide used clothing, food, and teach us basic English. I recall one particular English teacher who came over to our apartment on most nights and helped us with English. On our last day in Atlanta, she gave me a gold-plated dollar coin. To me, it symbolized the spirit of the American people. I don't know if she realized how that planted a seed in my heart that would grow into something wonderful later in my life. I was filled with joy due to her generosity.

Two years later our uncle located us and invited us to move to Los Angeles. There would be opportunity, he told us, and we would be close to one another. My uncle's home was a ten-minute walk from our apartment, and my mom found work in the garment factory. I got to work with my mom in the factory after school. My job would be to sew and press garments. I was paid up to 15 cents per piece. It was a typical sweatshop.

This routine of work and school went on for years until my mom gathered enough money to buy two donut shops and a garment business. At first, I was to work in one of the donut shops with my sisters, working around our school schedule. Mom operated the garment business, and my brother operated the other donut shop. All business operations were directed by my mom. They functioned well as long as we followed her directions without question.

With time – it grew more difficult. As I grew older I became more curious and confused about many things. These unanswered questions left a feeling of restlessness. I began to resist being under the strict control of my mother – who never offered an explanation for her demands. And I began to rebel.

As a result of my rebelliousness, I was physically beaten and not allowed to cry. I experienced emotional abuse from my mom, who told me I was worthless. The abuse continued well into my adulthood. I started to resent and hate my mom, my family, and life in general. You can well imagine how the experiences I endured in Cambodia and in my family system began to take their toll. As a result, I contemplated and attempted suicides.

Working at the donut shop one day, a customer introduced me to personal growth books. I became interested in the subject quickly, learning how to cope with my life history. I read many books from the library like *Seeds of Greatness* by Denis Waitley, *Leading an Inspired Life* by Jim Rohn, *The Psychology of Achievement* by Brian Tracy and *Think and Grow Rich* by Napoleon Hill.

As a result, I learned to build confidence and self-acceptance. I learned to love myself, even though my family doesn't have this language and have never said "I love you." I also discovered my uniqueness. I am expressive, inquisitive, sensitive, and I'd become "westernized." It had become harder for me to shift from my Western demeanor to Chinese with my family.

As Teochewnese – our personality is strong and adaptable. We are competitive and will not settle. Thus I've become quite enterprising.

I've owned and managed several different businesses, and I became a real estate investor. I thought that I would be happy once I was financially free. I thought if I had a luxury car and a home I would be loved and accepted. Surely mom would be proud. However, as it turned out, those were simply external values. I discovered I needed to work on my inner self.

While personal growth material and reading helped me to cope with my life issues and family system, it was no longer effective. I found myself crying to sleep most nights and on my knees praying, not knowing to whom or to what. I just cried out to the universe. Although my family believes in Buddha, follows the Buddhist tradition of offering food to our ancestors, and believes reincarnation is the way to Nirvana, nothing would assuage my inner wounds and the haunting memories.

I developed health challenges with Graves's Disease, nearly losing my sight. My thyroid gland was out of balance. I developed chronic fatigue and could not get out of bed. Unable to work, I lived on my savings and investments until they were exhausted.

Then I met Tessa. She shared her own life's struggles. Yet, I could see her face lit up with a countenance of peace. Her demeanor was of love and joy I had never seen in anyone before. As she spoke, her hope and zeal for life was palpable. I asked how she was able to have such peace and love in her life. She shared with me her story of Christ in her life. I wanted that.

I went to church that Sunday morning, Light and Life Christian Fellowship in Long Beach, California, and was greeted by a warm and loving Pastor, Dr. Larry Walkemeyer. The members of this loving church were equally happy and inviting. Everyone seemed genuinely joyful. I felt drawn to this church, I was wooed. I attended every Sunday, not letting my family know. This was my secret. Soon thereafter, Pastor Larry prayed for me, and I got baptized into this new faith. God's presence was palpable. I now have this love and joy – just like Tessa.

I kept my newfound faith from my family for years. Then I gathered enough courage to tell my mom how I had found happiness, peace and love in the Lord Jesus. She was not happy with this development and proclaimed that she was my god and we are Buddhists. Consequently, I was disowned by the family. Even though my relationship with my family became distant, I continued to pray for my family. I was saddened by the brokenness of our family and hoped they too would experience the love and peace I found.

After coming to my new faith, I began to take every opportunity to pray for healing of my health, for a breakthrough from the haunting memories, for a total restoration of my emotional well-being and most importantly, for me to forgive those who have wronged me.

I am now experiencing God's miracles in my life. My health has been restored. I am healed of Graves's Disease. According to recent blood tests, my thyroid gland is now normal. I have completely forgiven those who've wronged me, especially my mom.

I now experience God's unconditional love and the transformation within my own spirit and soul. God used many others to speak into my life. He disclosed my story and challenges from my childhood to those who prayed for me. I now know that God has been with me all of my life.

He protected me from the massive Killing Fields in the Khmer Rouge, and hid me from death and torture. He showed me kindness through what might seem like random acts of kindness from teachers or a friend at a seemingly insignificant donut shop. He gave me new friends like Tessa to show me where to find real friendship and love. I merely said "yes."

Today my family relationship is more functional. I now pray at my family dinner and am able to share my story with my sisters and brother. I am now having a healthier "adult" relationship with my mom. I have compassion and understanding for her challenges in the loss of her husband and three children. She risked her life almost every day – to give her children a better opportunity. I realized what a hero she is, and I have come to cherish her.

I was a part of a pilot group for a book of the women's workshop, *Beautifully Gifted*, led by author Dr. Angela Bisignano, I learned that my gift is to share my story to empower other women; that no matter what tribulation we experienced, we can rise above those circumstances through the power of forgiveness.

I can say that today, I am living my daily life victoriously through the power of forgiveness in Christ. I am finally free from the chains of bondage and past oppression, and I am now free to love and be loved.

About Jen

Jennifer Lee is the daughter of a long line of successful entrepreneurs from Southeast Asia. As a child her family had a thriving import and export business in China, Laos, Vietnam and Cambodia.

At seven years of age, her life was turned upside down. Her family lost their business, and she found herself in a Cambodian slave concentration camp. For the next four years, she and her family endured and survived the horrors of the Khmer Rouge/Pol Pot genocide.

After years of enduring the hardships and cruelty of refugee camps, her family was given sponsorship to come to America by a local church group. They arrived in Atlanta Georgia. As a teen, Jennifer learned to adapt to a new culture, a new language, and ultimately found a new faith.

Having the courage to be unique and to pursue her own dreams, Jennifer became a successful entrepreneur and business consultant. Continuing the family legacy of entrepreneurship, Jennifer continues to pursue her passion in business as well as business consulting.

For the first time, she now tells her story of overcoming the odds of having lived through the tragedy of having lost her father and three siblings to the Killing Fields. She shares her story of love and forgiveness as a way toward healing of the deep wounds. She shares her deep religious convictions as the basis for her own healing and strength. Jennifer motivates women everywhere. For women who have gone through their own life struggles – she inspires others to pursue their uniqueness and calling in life.

Jennifer pursued her Business Administration degree in Entrepreneurship from California State University of Los Angeles.

Jennifer remains an active member with Toastmasters International, and continues to help others by volunteering through various organizations such as South Bay Literacy Council, American Red Cross, Cerritos Performing Arts, Long Beach International City Theater as well as a Volunteer Coordinator and Hospice Consultant for Tower Hospice.

Jennifer's desire is to return one day to Cambodia to build a Christian school that provides free education to both children and adults and spread the Gospel, as well as to share the spirit of entrepreneurship.

Connect with Jennifer...
Email: JLee@JLee4Success.com
Twitter: www.twitter.com/jlee4success.com
Website: www.JLee4Success.com
Facebook: www.facebook.com/JLee4Success

CHAPTER 7

DOMINATE OR DISAPPEAR —
7-STEP POWER PRINCIPLE S-Y-S-T-E-M

BY LISA MACQUEEN

Anybody who wants to succeed in business knows it doesn't just happen. It doesn't matter what products or services you sell. It doesn't even matter what size your business is. The cold hard truth of it is if you want to make more money, you can't compete with others in your market. Why? Because when you compete, what you're really doing is mixing down at the lowest common denominator – the price. If you're obscure in your market, your price, value and package doesn't matter – because you don't stand out – your prospects don't know you. However, when you dominate a market, when people know who you are, you can charge more, have more credibility and be more visible as an industry leader.

I've always loved the idea of having my own business, but for the first part of my career, I was happy in my cushy sales and marketing position with a large hotel chain. Travelling the world, regular pay, great conditions, and customers who absolutely loved what I was selling – in fact, I never felt like I was selling anything to them – gorgeous hotels in fabulous locations – sure!

In short… in anyone's world – a dream job.

So imagine that moment when my husband asked me to come and join him in our family business – an office cleaning business that, by the way, wasn't doing particularly well.

I was torn. I loved my job, the people I worked with and all the great perks – but I knew that if we really wanted to enjoy financial freedom and success, the two of us joining forces would be the quickest route to achieving those goals.

So I jumped in and joined Cleancorp, and it was a steep learning curve. I had to learn pretty fast how to sell something that nobody really wants to buy. I mean, let's face it; it's hard to get excited about purchasing a cleaning contract when all you want is a clean home or office… I had to learn how to sell something that's not very social or sexy – no one goes into the bathroom at work and thinks "wow, this bathroom is clean, I'm going to post a pic on Instagram, send a tweet out and put an update on Facebook,"…right? So, coming up with unique ways to promote and position our business became my No.1 objective.

In the process I learnt 7 things. These are seven things which, if you do them well, will ensure that your business will continue to grow week-after-week, month-after- month and year-after-year. I call these steps my *7-STEP POWER PRINCIPLE S-Y-S-T-E-M (Save Your Self Time, Energy and Money)*, and by doing these seven things really well, I took our business from a struggling mess with no systems or processes, to a multi-million dollar national business in just a few short years; so if a cleaning business that isn't sexy and is selling a service that no one really wants to buy can do it, then I assure you, this system will work for you too.

POWER PRINCIPLE STEP #1 -
YOU HAVE TO FIND THE RIGHT TRIBE

Let me be clear here – when it comes to attracting prospects to your business, you need to make sure you're getting your message to your **ideal** clients – your tribe. I can't emphasise this point enough - you can't be all things to all people. If you try to market to everyone, your product or service won't really appeal to anyone – you need to be thinking in terms of targeting a niche that you can dominate.

Your ideal clients are a group of people or businesses who will give you the best return on your investment, they will be easy to work with, they'll stay with you the longest, and they'll spend the most with you over the longest period of time. They'll also be happy to refer your business or service to their friends and associates, and write you testimonials...

Doing your research is the fastest way to find out who's a good fit for you and your business. Take a look at your existing clients: Who pays on time, is pleasant to deal with, appreciates your service and efforts, and refers you to friends and colleagues. Chances are, they are your ideal client and therefore your target market. Go talk to them! Ask them why they like doing business with you – what is it about your product or service that they like, what are the 'wants' that you are fulfilling for them? Imagine what your business and revenues would look like if you knew how to attract more customers like that?

Then compare them to other clients you currently do business with – perhaps they are difficult, maybe even punishing, to work with – they always want the lowest price, then pay you late, they're always complaining or sending things back, and they're never satisfied no matter what you do or say? Working with clients like that is a huge drain on any business and likely costing you a lot of money.

Remember that the reason a client is going to do business with you is to satisfy some want or need they have. Your product or service must solve some problem in their lives. If you find out what their needs and wants are, and then fill them better than anyone else, you will dominate your market.

POWER PRINCIPLE STEP #2 -
IDENTIFY THEIR "HOT BUTTONS"

If you want success – you have to get attention! Once you've figured out who your ideal client is, then you need to create your marketing messages around their 'hot buttons.' Hot buttons are the problems, frustrations and concerns that matter most to people as they consider doing business with you – so what problem are you trying to solve? For example, in the case of a plumber, a few hot buttons would be – (a) Be on time, (b) Be honest and (c) Fix it fast, etc.

In the case of my cleaning business, the hot buttons for our ideal clients are – consistency, reliability, security, and high attention to detail. So, our marketing is created around providing solutions to those problems.

Remember, to be significant and to dominate in your market, you've got to be unique and different – and then focus attention on those differences by showing your prospects why they're important – using social media is an awesome way to get this started, as well as landing pages, websites, webinars, etc.

POWER PRINCIPLE STEP #3 -
LEAD GENERATION AND CAPTURE

This Power Principle is critical to your success. Once you've identified who you want in your tribe, and what their hot buttons are, with highly-targeted marketing you'll begin to attract more prospects. The next step then, is how do you capture your leads?

Lead generation is complex - I'd need a whole book to write fully on this subject; however, there are some very successful strategies for lead-gen such as offering a free e-book, a free report, free webinars, etc. in return for a name and email address. The lead generation tool will typically be something which will be of interest to your target audience, and this will appear on your website, Facebook page, landing pages, advertisements etc.

This strategy works irrespective of whether your prospect is ready to buy right now or not, because it gives you an opportunity to build a relationship with them, to get that prospect to know, like and trust you, and to build value in the eyes of the prospect, by providing them with helpful information or insights on your product or service.

POWER PRINCIPLE STEP #4 –
AUTOMATION LEADS TO DOMINATION

If you don't already use automation in your business, now is the time to change. (Disclaimer alert: I'm the 2014 Winner of the Infusionsoft Small Business ICON Award, as well as being a Certified Partner – so I love this platform.) Regardless of my bias though, to grow a business which is scalable, you need to leverage your time.

In the early days with Cleancorp, when we won a new client, I'd type up the new contract, put a welcome kit together, type up the label for the envelope, drive to the post office and stand in line to mail the package – it would take me roughly an hour to do all that. Then, I'd hope the client would sign and return it to me. If they didn't, I'd have to go through all of that again. Not a good use of my time, and not very predictable results.

Today, when a client says 'yes', I can literally do all of that in a few minutes – with no visit to the post office. The whole process is automated from start to finish; I'm using automation to leverage my time so I get time back into my day to get on with other things.

POWER PRINCIPLE STEP #5 –
THE PERSONAL TOUCHES

I love receiving packages in the mail. I don't know why this excites me, but the fact is, receiving something unexpectedly is, well, fun.

I recently purchased a book online through an author's website – a fairly standard transaction, that is, until the book arrived two days later, hand- addressed. When I opened the package, the book was beautifully gift wrapped, with ribbon, and a hand written card from the author, telling me that she hoped I'd enjoy reading it (which I did).

Now, she could have had a fulfilment house ship it to me, and I still would have been happy with the book, but chances are I wouldn't have been sharing this story with you now. You see, that personalised interaction left an impression on me – she cared that I purchased her book, and she made an effort to make sure it would be enjoyable to not only read, but to receive.

So the point here is, it's all about the customer experience. How can you show your clients and customers that you care about them and their business and in the process, win a raving fan? It could be something as simple as a hand written thank you card, remembering when their birthday is, or seeing an article you think they'd enjoy reading, cutting it out and sending it to them. The point is, you're thinking about them – small gestures like these resonate, and they won't cost you the earth to do.

POWER PRINCIPLE STEP #6 -
HOW TO UPSELL AND GET REFERRALS
AND TESTIMONIALS

Success loves preparation. So if you've followed my Power Principles, you will have attracted your ideal client, your tribe, who will know, like and trust your company, and you'll be fulfilling their needs and wants, their 'hot buttons,' adding value and keeping in contact using personal touches along the way. If you're doing all of this, your clients will want more from you.

At this point, you should be offering choices to them that will enhance your product or service. For example, if you're offering Website Design Services, then a natural upsell could be something like copywriting services, or ghost writing services, and then once the website is live, the next step could be to offer them SEO services or pay per click. Listen to what your customers say, and when you hear something that is a pain, frustration or concern for them, think about how you can use these new 'hot buttons' to upsell your services.

The greatest compliment you can get from a Customer or Client is when they refer you to others. Referrals are a big part of building your business and it's important to have some strategies in place to make this process work for both your client or customer, and the person they referred to you.

Have you ever given a referral and heard nothing? You wouldn't rush to give another would you? Recognition is essential when you receive a referral - thank the person who sent the referral your way (I like to send a personalised card with cookies). You should also contact the person they've referred you to as soon as possible, and set up a time to meet, or a discovery call as soon as you can. Remember that referral business has a much lower customer acquisition cost, so you can afford to spend more time with them to educate and inform them. One little thing I like to do is send out a Tweet to thank them for their time and interest – if your client or customer is a business owner, they'll appreciate the mention.

If you think it will work with your tribe, perhaps a financial incentive would be a great way to get referrals – this could be in the form of gift cards or vouchers that both referrer and referee are given if the deal goes through (you will need to check with each company's policy on this, as some organisations don't allow these type of schemes).

Remember, referrals are something that you should be asking for on an on-going basis. The best time to ask for a referral is after something really great has happened – for example, if you shipped an order in double quick time, called to follow up and the client tells you how happy they were to get it that quickly – that's a great time to ask for a referral. If they can't think of anyone at that moment in time, then suggest they write you a testimonial instead – a few lines on how much they like dealing with your company, or the fantastic changes they've experienced since switching to your company – that will add credibility for your business when seen in marketing materials and on your website, and help you dominate your market.

POWER PRINCIPLE STEP #7 – TAKE ACTION

Have you heard the saying that knowledge = power? It's really only half true, because it's the *application* of knowledge that gives you the real power – the steps that you take on a consistent basis to grow your business.

When I first started working with a mentor, she said to me *"Lisa, you can either be committed to your own success or you can be interested. The difference is that when you are committed, you'll do what it takes. If you are only interested, you'll do what is convenient."*

My wish for you as an entrepreneur, is that you will not be satisfied with average – average is the 'death zone' for business because when your marketing and advertising looks exactly like everyone else's, prospects can't easily determine the real value you provide. If they can't find a distinction, they'll always go to the lowest price as a differentiator.

When you dominate a market – when you have the right messages going to the right people, addressing their concerns and frustrations and offering smart solutions, then the magic happens. When the value you offer exceeds the price, then people will pay you money, and you will dominate the market rather than disappear in it.

About Lisa

Lisa Macqueen helps her clients crack the code of small business success by using a combination of technology and smart marketing ideas to dominate their industry. She spent 20 years working in sales and marketing for large international hotel chains, before joining her husband, Hamish, in the family business, Cleancorp. Not long after starting her 'new career' she realised that not only was the business struggling, but also there were no systems or processes in place to capture leads, nurture clients or manage day-to-day workflow. So, she set about creating her *7-Step Power Principle S-y-s-t-e-m* (Save Yourself Time, Energy and Money), and turned the cleaning business into a multi-million dollar national cleaning company in the space of a few short years.

Lisa's new career is centred around her philosophy that "automation leads to domination," and her goal is to help her clients build a relationship with their prospects and customers, because when people know who you are, you can charge more, have more credibility and be more visible as an industry leader. Essentially, you can dominate markets instead of competing in them.

Lisa is also the winner of the Infusionsoft Small Business ICON Award for 2014 (formerly known as the Ultimate Marketer Award). She is an entrepreneur, speaker, author, marketer, business owner, wife and mother to three daughters.

You can connect with Lisa at:
lisa@creativeautomation.com.au
www.twitter.com/MacqueenLisa
https://www.facebook.com/lisa.macqueen.77
www.automationqueen.com

CHAPTER 8

THE ROAD TO HAPPINESS AND ENLIGHTENMENT

BY LUCY LIU

Is it possible to be in a state of bliss, freedom, love and optimal health no matter what happens in your life? Yes! My story will tell you that it is absolutely possible.

Picture this: More than ten years ago I gave up my comfortable life and demanding job as a petroleum chemical engineer working in the largest petroleum company in China and came to this wonderful country as an immigrant. I started my new life journey as a student at McGill University to study Nutrition, something that I had been longing to do for a long time. I had asked myself why I chose uncertainty. It was my passion, my soul desire and my dreams that pushed me to take challenges and to be uncomfortable.

ADVENTURES IN CHILDHOOD

I love adventures. When I was 6 years old, with my great imagination, I jumped off from the roof with two umbrellas thinking they were two parachutes, and I was an aviator! Luckily I was smart enough to choose a short shed and that didn't break my legs. One day I climbed up a big tree to check the cosy nests for birds, I was curious what was going on with the bird's families and how they have the babies. Of course they didn't appreciate the invader; their angry cries and outrageous flying almost scared me off the tree. The adventures in my childhood life have embedded the seeds for taking risks and uncertainties later on in my life.

OVERCOMING AN EATING DISORDER

I never discussed my eating disorder with my parents. Not only because they don't understand, but also they love me so much that they would worry all the time. The early onset of my eating disorder was when I was 13 years old. I was not overweight, but I was fascinated by those beautiful movie stars and models in magazines. I dreamt about having a slim and tall body. The thought became the action, I started to starve myself. When I was too hungry and had an urge to eat, I purged out the foods with intention after I ate. When my eating disorder became a chronic condition, I started to hate myself, my mood was low and I lived in my own shadow. I isolated myself and was afraid of social connections with classmates and friends at school with the fear that they may find out. I lived in my own small world that was filled with hopelessness, struggling and fear. My physical health went downhill. One time I was so skinny that I was less than 90 lbs. My menstrual periods stopped, I had trouble sleeping, and I had no energy.

This chronic eating disorder dragged me through university to my new career as a chemical engineer. Worse than that, I didn't have the desire for romance. I didn't have close friends and I was jealous about other young ladies' healthy looks and energetic bodies. The fantasy to have a body image like a star or model did not attract me anymore. Deep inside, I was yearning for a normal life, I wanted romance, and I wanted a social life. It was the deep desire that I wanted to feel better and I wanted to get healthier that caused me to take actions and I was ready in my early 20s. Within 2 years, I completely recovered from my eating disorder that I was battling with for almost 10 years with no relapse afterwards. It affected me so deeply mentally and emotionally that I still dreamt about having an eating disorder long after I recovered. It was my strong will and determination that I wanted to get healthy and I wanted to have a better life that created the miracle. After I overcame my eating disorder, I started to eat healthy, developed a social life and exercised regularly; also I became more and more interested in nutrition. Later, I reflect that the root causes of my eating disorder were underlying self-esteem issues and lack of confidence. I used to live under others' shadows; my own value was from the validation of others. I did well in school, which marked the real self-esteem issues when it comes to social connections and human relationships.

> *Being worthy isn't something you earn,*
> *it's something you recognize.*
> ~ Mike Dooley

Today I love and appreciate my body like my best friend. My eating disorder not only changed my concept about a healthy body image, but also brought in more dreams and passion into my life.

FOLLOWING MY DREAMS AND PASSION

After I graduated from high school, my father chose the career for me because my father was in the petroleum field for many years; he thought that was the best career at that time. I love chemistry, I love those 3-dimensional atoms and structures and they are like arts fascinating me. The fantasy becomes a fuel for study; and my chemistry was ranked as No. 1 in the entire high school, which made me proud of becoming a chemical engineer. However, after I graduated from the university and started training in my new career, life painted different pictures for me, I was climbing those grey towers with no excitement at all, they seemed so tall that I was climbing a huge mountain. Those fit-all uniforms were killing my feminine side as a woman. I felt bored and tired at work. Worse than that, I had headaches sitting in front of computers drawing flow charts for towers and pipes. My health conditions went down again, I felt sick from time to time, either with headaches or sore throats.

In order to take care of my health and feel better, I studied Chinese herbal medicine, diet and nutrition. My book shelf was filled with diet books and herbal medicine, the more I read the more I was fascinated about it.

Thoughts became desires and desires became actions. Finally, I made a big decision that shocked everyone in my family. The decision was that I was going to give up my career and immigrate to Canada and change my life completely. My poor mother cried and begged me not to leave the country, and my father and sisters were all silent. However, the seeds were embedded since I was a kid that nothing could stop me from my dreams and adventures.

Sometimes the things you are most afraid of are the things that make you the happiest. I left the fear behind and started my new journey. I had no clue what was going to happen. The night I landed in Montreal, a stranger who my friend had introduced and who was supposed to pick me up didn't show up on time. I struggled to balance myself pushing a cart loaded with luggage like a small hill. In fact, the cart carried me left and right along the hall way to the exit. It was at the end of October, when I looked outside, it was dark and raining and I felt chilly. I was scared and my heart was suspended in the air. Just at the moment I was wondering, a smiling lady approached me and said "Bonjour" in French, which is "Hello" in English. At that time, I didn't know a single word in French, to me it sounded totally alien, and I interpreted it in Chinese based on its pronunciation as "stupid pig!" My heart beat faster and I felt embarrassed. I pretended I didn't see her. Then I saw a public phone on the wall beside me and my eyes sparked with hope that I could call the person who was supposed to pick me up. So I rushed to the phone and put two dollars in the slot, then dialled the number I had in my pocket. Again, another shock, the strange French message from the phone totally freaked me out. I was nervous and my hands were shaking with panic. Just at this moment, I saw a Chinese face outside the door. A man walked towards the door. My instinct told me that he was the one to pick me up, I waved my hands at him just like I saw a life saver. Sure enough, he picked me up. From that moment, I have learned that adventures can be scary too. Even today I still joke about the pronunciation of "Bonjour."

A few days later after I landed in Montreal, I used the public transportation to get to know the city. I got lost on the street. Not only because all the road signs in French were unreadable to me, but also my broken English didn't make sense to others either. Again, luck knocked on my door and a stranger took me home in his car.

FIGHTING AGAINST CANCER

After moving many times in Montreal and Ontario for training and work, I finally landed in my dream location – BC (British Columbia) – working as a clinical dietitian a few years ago. However, the excitement was replaced with another scare. I was diagnosed with thyroid cancer with a nodule on my neck, I had a similar nodule before, but was not fully treated and this time was a recurrent one! Two months after I moved to BC, I had surgery, followed by a full month of radiation treatment. Lying on the operating bed for the surgery, my mind was very peaceful, many moments in the past played like a movie in my head; I told myself, "I have the power to overcome this!" I didn't tell anyone at work and used up all my vacation for treatment. I lost my voice and couldn't eat during the treatment, I still had a bad sore throat after the treatment, but I went back to work on time. I was working more than one job at that time, trying to build a better future. The busy schedule at work eased my pain in my mind and soul. The deep desire that I wanted to be cancer free and have an optimal health condition brought me into another field: Alternative medicine, which opened another opportunity to me not only to heal myself, but also opened a new window to look at health care solutions. Many times I asked myself what was the root cause for my thyroid cancer? Why had that happened to me? After years diving into alternative medicine and Chinese medicine, I came to a conclusion that everything happens for a reason. On the surface, my thyroid cancer may be related to hormone imbalances that can be tracked down from the eating disorder I had before, but the root cause is related to self-love and self-control.

I do believe that the single most important thing
I could ever share with you with regard to maximizing
the health, harmony, and happiness in your life can be
summed up in just two words: 'Love Yourself'.
~ Mike Dooley

BOUNCING BACK FROM RELATIONSHIP BREAKUPS

I believe that relationships are for us to learn and grow. The last ex-boyfriend I had suddenly left me a few years ago, I was shocked and depressed, I had such an emotional distress that I couldn't eat and sleep for a few weeks, and lost 8 lbs in two weeks. That was the biggest depression I had had in my life, it took me more than three months to struggle back to my normal life. One day, I was driving while listening to the radio, and I heard the topic of "how to create a happy life?" I was asking myself, "What is happiness?" No answer. Then I asked myself another question, "What is the purpose of my life?" No answer. I started to think what was the very last thing left when I let go of those attachments – family and the loved ones? It is my independence, who I am at the very core that no one can take away. I started to realize that I was missing the most important thing in my life – happiness. I made a commitment that I was going to live in a place that I felt happy for no reason and love for no reason. I was craving so much for happiness that I started to read books and listen to the seminars about self-development. Then the person who left me came back to my life. I took him back because I still loved him deeply at that time. However, after a year of self-learning for relationships and self growth, finally I realized that I deserved a better relationship and a better life! I decided to leave that unfulfilled relationship even though I cared for and loved that person very much.

I will never forget the moment I made the decision to leave the relationship; I was driving down the road to work, crying and yelling loudly to myself "I will NEVER have a heart-broken breakup again!" I was yelling this sentence to myself for a few times, and surprisingly, it worked! I felt the sky was brighter and the trees beside the road were more vivid and vibrant, I felt less pain in my heart and I recovered very fast. Within two months I moved on smoothly and stayed positive, every day I reinforced myself to become happier and more confident.

> *You have to remember that freedom is the highest value,*
> *and if love is not giving you freedom then it is not love.*
> ~ Osho

OPTIMAL HEALTH SOLUTIONS

My career is also climbing to new heights! It has been my dream to have my own business. After my own self-healing experiences and years diving into alternative medicine, I have realized that drugs cannot improve our health conditions and only treat symptoms. Finally, I launched my online business, it is my passion and dream to combine conventional medicine and alternative medicine as a holistic approach for health care, creating harmony between the mind and body – as the whole is greater than the sum of the parts. I want to use my knowledge, my experience and gifts to assist others to achieve optimal health and maintain successful, long–lasting, healthy life-style changes.

It is all coming from a place of self-love and deservedness. Today my health is at its best. I take care of myself physically, mentally, emotionally and spiritually. Every day I wake up with gratitude and joy and I am taking inspired actions to fulfill my passion and live my dream life. In fact, all the challenges in life are great opportunities to bring us to a higher level of awakening and enlightenment. I am blessed with everything that has happened in my life. It has made me a strong, confident, successful, optimistic and independent person. Looking towards the future, my life is getting better and better!

Last but not the least, I would like to take this opportunity to inspire others and help others, and make this world a better place to live!

"There is no path to happiness. Happiness is the path."
~ Buddha

About Lucy

As the founder of optimalhealthsolutions.ca, Lucy Liu's mission is to assist others to achieve optimal health and create a life that is full of happiness, abundance, good health and wellness. Lucy has developed a holistic approach to help others by creating harmony between the mind and body. Lucy works on the body as a whole. Her unique approach for health solutions is based on her philosophy that optimal health is the alignment of emotional health, physical health, mental health and spiritual health. When all these components are in harmony; a blissful state of optimal health can be achieved and maintained. Lucy values health as the greatest wealth, because it is the foundation of happiness, abundance and loving relationships.

Lucy started a career as a Chemical Engineer in a top petroleum company in Asia in her early 20s, but she soon found out that was not her life's dream, she is fascinated about health, nutrition, Chinese medicine and alternative medicine. With her passion, she went back to school at McGill University, one of the top universities in North America, to study nutrition. After graduation, Lucy worked as a clinical dietitian for different health care facilities. With years of work experience to help clients and patients improve their health conditions and achieve the best outcome, Lucy has developed many specialities in health fields including weight loss, eating disorders, mental health and chronic diseases management, etc.

Lucy has not only established a widely-recognized reputation in health and nutrition, but also achieved success in many fields including *Internationally Certified Master Hypnotist, Master NLP (Neuro-linguistic programming) Practitioner, Advanced Law of Attraction Practitioner and Life Coach;* also as *Certified Advanced Theta Healing Practitioner, Reiki Practitioner, Akashic Records Practitioner* and *Numerologist.* In addition, Lucy also has in-depth knowledge in Chinese medicine.

After years of experience serving patients and clients as a Clinical Dietitian, Lucy has devoted herself to bringing a holistic approach, which combines Western medicine, Chinese medicine and Alternative medicine together, to help clients and patients achieve the optimum outcome. With her passion and dreams, she successfully launched her online business – optimalhealthsolutions.ca – to help others overcome obstacles in their lives, leverage their gifts and talents, fulfill their deep desires, create a life that they desire and maintain long-term success for healthy life-style changes.

Lucy is also a well known author and speaker. She has been invited to speak to many special groups and college students in various topics regarding health and nutrition. Lucy also published many blogs about Holistic Health, Women's Health, Children's Health, Functional Foods, Healing Foods and Natural Remedies, Anti-aging Solutions, Weight Loss, Fitness Training and Sports Nutrition as well as Happiness projects. Her approach is to dig into the root causes of illnesses and sub-optimal health conditions, and provide a broad range of solutions from Herbal medicine, Energy medicine, Holistic nutrition and many other healing modalities to help others achieve the best outcomes. For more information, please visit her website: http://optimalhealthsolutions.ca

You can connect with Lucy at:
Email: Lucyliu@optimalhealthsolutions.ca
Facebook: https://www.facebook.com/optlucyliu
Twitter: https://twitter.com/opt_solutions_
LinkedIn: https://www.linkedin.com/in/lucyliu8

CHAPTER 9

PROCESS YIELDS PROGRESS

BY NICK NANTON

The journey of a thousand miles
begins with a single step.
~ Lao Tzu

I am willing to bet that almost every single one of you reading this chapter has read the above quote – or had it quoted to you – in the course of your life. You're starting college and it's rough –somebody tells you about that first step. You're having trouble getting a new business off the ground – somebody tells you about the first step.

Whenever you're at the initial stage of anything – you hear about 'that thousand miles' and 'that first step'. And to be fair, you can't argue with it – it's true. That 'thousand mile journey' starts with that first step.

What people don't discuss, however, is the 4,634[th] step. Or the 5,489[th] step. When you're so far from the beginning that you're in danger of forgetting where you're going – and when you're still so far from the end, you think you'll never make it there.

When you're in the middle of the grind – when it feels like the pay-off will never come – and when you may be so tired you don't think there ever will be a pay-off – that's when it can be incredibly difficult (maybe the most difficult) to take the next step.

I firmly believe that when you get to that tough slog where it just feels' like you're grinding it out for no reason', that's actually when you're in the middle of the real hard work that's going to ultimately validate your efforts. This is when it's most important to follow through on the process and systems you've set up – and not forget what got you as far as you already are. That's when you need to power through with your process and get what you originally wanted with it.

But let's not start with the 5,489th step. Let's take Lao Tzu's advice and start with the first.

THE FIRST STEP AND WHY IT'S CRUCIAL

Someone who I recently learned of, and am enamored with, has become an inspiration to me and a whole lot of other people, …former UCLA basketball coach John Wooden. He always had an interesting first step for his players at his 'first talk' of the season. It probably wasn't so interesting for the seniors to hear the exact same 'first talk' they heard when they were freshman - but Wooden was a man who believed in the proper process, which is one big reason he was voted, "Coach of the Century" by ESPN.

That first talk of the season was not about the goals for the team, who the captains would be, or any of the usual rally cries of a typical coach,nope, it was all about Wooden demonstrating, in meticulous detail, how the players should properly put on their socks and their shoes. Yes, he would actually show them how to do it. And yes, you usually don't get that kind of instruction after you're two or three years old – especially from one of the best college coaches of all time. Frankly, most coaches at any level above elementary school would think it was too trivial to deal with – and college boys should know how to dress themselves!

Wooden, however, knew that most good players ended up on the bench because they ended up with blisters from game play. And he knew most of those blisters could be prevented *if players would simply take the time and put on their socks and shoes correctly.*

Hence the lecture every year – even to the players who had already heard it!! It was a vital first step to Wooden's process – and do you really argue with a guy who ended up with an over-80% win record? ...who won ten national championships? ...who is regarded as America's 'winningest' coach? I certainly wouldn't!

By building from that base, Wooden created teams that knew basketball inside and out. He gave them a process that enabled them to do their very best – and turned him into a legendary coach.

It's what all of us need to do in our individual businesses. Your first steps, in any venture, should be about finding out what works, from the bottom up. 'Fine-tuning' will obviously come as you continue along the way, but if you nail down the process that works for you personally, it's a template that can take you to where you want to go – *if you learnt the basics, remember them and continue to implement them.*

Some aspects of that process are generic – they're essential to anyone trying to do what you're doing. Others are personal – making use of your specific talents and what works best for you. Out of all of it, however, you build your own unique process by seeing what's effective and what isn't. Once you have it all put together, you drill that process into your brain at every given opportunity. And you never forget why you use the process you use – because it works ...for you! No, not for the guy down the street, or somebody two office doors down from yours...but for YOU!!!!

And it has to be the process that's going to serve you all the way down the line. I have to hand it to my four year-old son Brock's T-ball coach, Coach Will, because he showed me this power principle in action and how it's relevant at any age.

The kid that was playing pitcher (no, really, in T-ball they have one, they just don't actually pitch!) in the game ran from the pitcher's mound to run down another kid running to home plate – and pulled it off. He got the out. But the coach told the pitcher that's not what he wanted to see. That's not how the game is played. It'll work out in T-ball, but that play won't work when the kids get a little older, and a little faster. He said, "You might get an out this year with that play, but we're not here to get outs, we're here to learn how to play baseball." Wow! Now that's what I'm talking about! Coach Will wanted them to learn how to play the right way for the long run – not just what worked for now – so as they moved on, they could power through with the proper process.

With any first steps, you should be doing the same thing – finding out how whatever "game" you're learning works, and how best to play it -whether it's the game of life, the game of business, or a true game. *The principle is the same.*

THE FIRST STEP AND WHY IT'S OVERRATED

No, I'm not getting into an argument with myself, it's true…first steps are absolutely crucial and also amazingly easy!

First of all, people are always incredibly encouraging when you start something new (unless they know you well enough to sense you're heading for disaster). It's exciting to them and they live vicariously through you trying something for the first time. Why? Because you have to do all the hard work and all they have to do is watch!

Seriously, how many quotes and advice do you see on beginning something, whether it's a business or a relationship or just a workout regimen? Whereas, when you're in the middle of something and whining about it – well, everybody's in the middle of something and whining about it. And they'd rather listen to themselves whine than listen to you do it!

The first step also often means *you're not putting that much at stake.* There's not a lot invested in it emotionally, physically or financially yet. It's basically setting a goal and beginning to figure out how you can achieve that goal.

Taking that first step usually means:

- You're beginning something you want to get done.
- You haven't faced serious opposition to your goal.

- You've psyched yourself up to get going – so you're 'pumped' to see it through.

- Nobody expects a lot from you – because you're just beginning to find out how it's done.

In other words, sure, you're nervous – but you're okay to start that long 'thousand mile' journey, whatever it is. It's not so bad. You're choosing to do it. And nobody will be too hard on you about it.

The first step is also generally not that complicated. Remember what the first day of school or a class was like? It was the teacher telling you what you were going to be doing the rest of the semester or year and that's about it. You didn't have to worry, at that point, about having homework done or passing any tests. You were just there – trying to stay awake until the bell rang. Hey, even with Coach Wooden, all they had to do was figure out how to put on their socks and shoes the first time he talked to them! Most of us can handle that kind of pressure.

And one last thing about the first step not really being all that bad – you can totally 'bail' before the second step. Seriously, most things won't have horrible consequences if you bail early (guys, this is not an excuse – the day after that bachelor party, don't even think about it!). Maybe you say to yourself, "Hey, I want to learn Mandarin Chinese." (I use this example in honor of Lao Tzu.) You take that first step – maybe you get an introduction to a beginner's Mandarin Chinese book – and then the bolt of lightning hits your brain…."Hey! This is hard! I'd rather spend the effort on _____." (You fill in the blank with your next goal).

What did you lose? …that $9.99 you spent on the book? …and those ten minutes it took you to realize it was hard enough for you to learn English? …let alone this.

Taking one step on the thousand mile journey and changing your mind? No big deal. Getting five hundred miles down the road and changing your mind? Enormous deal. That's why you can't…

DON'T JUST MUDDLE THROUGH THE MIDDLE

So let's talk about being five hundred miles down that thousand mile road. That's what I like to call the unsung hero of heroic struggles – the middle.

They say the closer you get to the summit, the harder it is to reach it. I've chosen to consciously disagree, and you can too with the right mindset – and I talked about this a little at the beginning of this chapter. When you're so far along, you forgot why you started - but you're not far enough to see where you're going - it's easy to feel like you're stumbling around in the dark, going through the motions, and completely not getting anywhere.

And that's where you have to power through with your process. That's where you have to put your socks and shoes on correctly and keep doing what you're doing, if you've proven to yourself that it works. You may need some adjustments – that's normal, because the world is always changing – but in general, you have to 'keep on keeping on.'

I'm speaking from personal experience on that point. For example, a big part of our business involves me speaking at different events all across the country. They are great because they usually generate a lot of interest in our business and we get to build a list of prospects who were interested enough to come out and hear me, and give us their contact information to stay in touch – so it's almost always a good decision to accept invitations to speak at events. It's something I've learned works for us and it's definitely a big part of my process.

Well, I was invited to speak at what was billed as a major seminar event in California – and I was told there might be a lot of influential people there that would be interested in doing business, and many of them had very large fan bases (sounds good, but believe me, I've heard it before and the delivery of those elements is usually far less than what has been promised). So I thought about it. It was a big commitment (a week in California, away from my family in Orlando), and a big financial commitment (not that it was overly expensive for the trip, but because of my marketing budget at the time, I had to choose between this trip and a new marketing campaign I really wanted to launch).

The California trip, more and more, just felt like a big hassle to me, and an inconvenient one at that. I was ready to skip it, when I remembered that this kind of thing – speaking at places where I could widen my circle of influence and boost my network – was really a vital way that we grow our business. So, I agreed to it.

When I got there, I was amazed at the number of top-tier speakers and writers that were in attendance – it was a room of about 100 people who were all seven figure speakers and authors. I won't drop names, but I would be willing to bet you'd know at least half of the people in the room. We're talking about men and women who literally fill STADIUMS with rabid fans wanting to hear them speak, and others who had collectively sold over 100 MILLION books! It was insane! Don't get me wrong, the seminar was hard work – sessions night and day – but out of that came lots of things, including an invitation to speak at another event which proved to be a huge windfall, and there are many other opportunities still being fleshed out, all because I didn't forget my **basic principles**, even when I was reluctant, and **I powered through my process.**

PROP-UP YOUR PROCESS WITH PRINCIPLES

When I was thinking about whether or not to accept that speaking engagement, I didn't think about making important new contacts or generating more business. I concentrated on the expense, the work and the inconvenience. Obviously, big mistake on my part. Fortunately, I got back on my thousand-mile road because I remembered that the processdidn't exist for its own sake – the process brought results!!!

*And that's what we all have to remember. We must continually perfect the process – and sticking to that process is more important than anything else...**because the process gets us to the goal line.***

When Coach Wooden gave his annual "socks and shoes speech," some older players would start to feel insulted that he was still teaching the ins and outs of footwear. They didn't want to listen to it all over again.

But consider this – do you think Coach Wooden really wanted to tell players how to put on their socks and shoes every single year?

Don't you think maybe one season, he said to himself, "Maybe I don't have to do this anymore. Maybe these college kids can figure this out for themselves." I'm willing to wager he did – and that he also went back to doing it because he once again realized that this was his process, it worked and he should stick to it. **...and because it was also important to his players' process.**

After the newness of whatever you're in the middle of wears off, it's tempting to forget all the building blocks that got you there. It's easy to be distracted by turn-offs on the thousand mile road and take another route ...that will take you somewhere you really don't want to go.

Both behaviors are dangerous to your business. Sticking to your the principles that you used to develop your process helps you avoid them. Maybe you have a choice between a lunch with somebody you like but isn't going to do much for your operation – and somebody else you don't know that well but could do an awful lot for you. You're better off seizing the second opportunity, even though you'll have to invest some time and energy in getting to know this person and selling them on you and your business.

Making productive choices that will further your process means you'll keep getting the results you want. And, hey, you can always have lunch with the other friend on a day when there isn't a conflict.

When the pay-off isn't necessarily in sight, you simply have to trust that what you're doing will work – and that your process will, in fact, see you through to the other side.

I will leave you with some very wise words from Coach Wooden: "Don't be too concerned with regard to things over which you have no control, because that will eventually have an adverse effect on things over which you have control."

You have control over what you do and how you do it. You can't control the outside factors. Even if you've made your process the most powerful it can be, it still won't work every single time. But if you fixate on the things that could go against you, you'll have a hard time achieving what you want to achieve.

Life is all about making the odds work in your favor – *and having a process that will allow you to power through to the end of whatever road you're on - which means that chances are you'll get what you're after.*

<u>So pull on those socks and lace up those shoes the right way – so you can win the game!</u>

About Nick

An Emmy Award-Winning Director and Producer, Nick Nanton, Esq., is known as the Top Agent to Celebrity Experts around the world for his role in developing and marketing business and professional experts, through personal branding, media, marketing and PR. Nick is recognized as the nation's leading expert on personal branding as Fast Company Magazine's Expert Blogger on the subject and lectures regularly on the topic at major universities around the world. His book *Celebrity Branding You®*, while an easy and informative read, has also been used as a text book at the University level.

The CEO and Chief StoryTeller at The Dicks + Nanton Celebrity Branding Agency, an international agency with more than 1800 clients in 33 countries, Nick is an award winning director, producer and songwriter who has worked on everything from large scale events to television shows with the likes of Steve Forbes, Brian Tracy, Jack Canfield (*The Secret, Chicken Soup for the Soul* Series), Michael E. Gerber, Tom Hopkins, Dan Kennedy and many more.

Nick is recognized as one of the top thought-leaders in the business world and has co-authored 30 best-selling books alongside Brian Tracy, Jack Canfield, Dan Kennedy, Dr. Ivan Misner (Founder of BNI), Jay Conrad Levinson (Author of the Guerilla Marketing Series), Super Agent Leigh Steinberg and many others, including the breakthrough hit *Celebrity Branding You!®*.

Nick has led the marketing and PR campaigns that have driven more than 1000 authors to Best-Seller status. Nick has been seen in *USA Today, The Wall Street Journal, Newsweek, BusinessWeek, Inc. Magazine, The New York Times, Entrepreneur® Magazine, Forbes,* FastCompany.com and has appeared on ABC, NBC, CBS, and FOX television affiliates around the country, as well as CNN, FOX News, CNBC, and MSNBC from coast to coast.

Nick is a member of the Florida Bar, holds a JD from the University Of Florida Levin College Of Law, as well as a BSBA in Finance from the University of Florida's Warrington College of Business. Nick is a voting member of The National Academy of Recording Arts & Sciences (NARAS, Home to The GRAMMYs), a member of The National Academy of Television Arts & Sciences (Home to the Emmy Awards), co-founder of the National Academy of Best-Selling Authors, a 16-time Telly Award winner, and spends his spare time working with Young Life, Downtown Credo Orlando, Entrepreneurs International and rooting for the Florida Gators with his wife Kristina and their three children, Brock, Bowen and Addison.

Learn more at:
www.NickNanton.com
www.CelebrityBrandingAgency.com

CHAPTER 10

THE CHOICE THAT MAKES ALL THE DIFFERENCE

BY JEFF YOUNG

This the last of human freedoms – to choose one's attitude in any given set of circumstances, to choose one's own way.
~ Dr. Victor Frankl

I sat across from Dr. Wilson who had examined the test results. Although we both wanted the news to be positive, if it were not, he would have to be the bad news bearer. Somehow it felt as if this news bearer had control over the results. I remember thinking, *Come on, Doc. Let's fix this thing and get this success train back on the tracks. Just say the word and everything will be alright.*

As a twenty-two year-old college student, I always took the earliest classes available, then immediately hit the library. All I wanted was to get my school responsibilities over and done with so I could get home to my guitar. Black 'n Blue guitarist, Jef "Woop" Warner, had taught me to play a couple years prior and I was obsessed. Music was way beyond a passion for me; it was the embodiment of why I lived. Woop and my brother Patrick had a record deal and were making industry connections daily. I had drive, vision, and a knack for reading tea leaves in the music industry. I knew what my life would be and how I would get there. Nothing could derail these well-laid plans – or so I thought. Something had gone awry in my ability to grip my guitar pick, and it was Dr. Wilson's job to get it figured out and ironed out. I had the future by the tail and a world to conquer, so this guitar pick nuisance would not do.

Doctor Wilson stared a hole through me as his lips parted, "The tests have all come back negative. There is no tumor or anything else blocking the neurological flow between your spinal cord and your extremities."

I sat silent before asking, "So what is causing this?"

Dr. Wilson remained calm, but his eyes and tone of voice conveyed an ominous message, "I think we're probably looking at ALS - Lou Gehrig's Disease." He then gave a detailed explanation of what it was I was facing.

Amyotrophic Lateral Sclerosis is a neurological disease whereby the nerve roots in your biological system progressively die off. The "Amyotrophic" part of the illness accounts for progressive weakness and deterioration of muscle tissue. The "Lateral Sclerosis" part of the malady accounts for distorted communication throughout the nervous system leading to severely impaired motor coordination. The disease progresses until only eyes and breathing muscles function. Death occurs when the muscles that support breathing function finally give out. I was told that there was no known cause, no cure, and medical science could do nothing for me. I could expect to spend the next three years dying a slow, horrifying death with no chance of help intervening.

It's been more than thirty years since that day in Dr. Wilson's office. I didn't die in the three years given, but today I cannot walk or lift my arms. My hands are almost completely useless, my speech is severely garbled, and I cannot fully fill my lungs with air. I am confined to a wheelchair and must fight through extreme mental, emotional, and physical barriers to carry out the simplest of life's functions. I tire easily, my neck and upper back fatigue and often serve me up extreme pain. All day I suffer from cramps in my fingers, toes, feet, legs, throat, and tongue. Every day this disease takes another piece of my life. And instead of conquering the world and having the future by the tail, it appears ALS has my world and future by the throat. But appearances can indeed be deceiving.

Life is about choices- career choices, choice of spouse, choosing how you will treat others, choosing to spend, save, or invest, deciding whether to get behind the wheel or to call a cab. The list of impacting choices and decisions that shape our circumstances and destinies is endless. But there is one choice that can make Heaven out of Hell, or Hell out of Heaven. That is your choice of the attitudes you decide to confront life with.

When I was told at age twenty-two that my dream was done, my life over, and to just get my affairs in order, I had a choice to make. I could curse God and spit at the world, or I could search for a way to turn this nightmare into something good. It took time and soul searching, but what I found was mind blowing. You cannot control what other people will do, say or think. You cannot change the past, and no matter how carefully you plan your future, you have absolutely no clue what tomorrow might bring. You can't stop time, the aging process, or your march toward death. You can build a castle of gold filled with treasure and it can be taken away. Marry an angel and they can turn devil, leave, or be taken from you. We are imperfect beings living in an unpredictable world, and you are fooling yourself if you think you can control all circumstances of your life. You have complete control of just one thing – your own thoughts. But that one thing is the linchpin of a life worth living.

The Oxford Dictionary defines **attitude** as: *a settled way of thinking or feeling about someone or something*. But how we feel about someone or something is based on what we think about them. And since we have the ability to choose our thoughts, we are responsible for our attitudes.

When this concept of controlling my thoughts and taking responsibility for my attitudes fully crystallized in my mind, my life changed. And I have never heard this concept put more aptly than by Charles Swindoll, Pastor of Stonebriar Community Church in Frisco, Texas:

"The longer I live, the more I realize the impact of attitude on life. Attitude to me is more important than facts. It is more important than the past, than education, than money, than circumstances, than failures, than successes, than what other people think, or say, or do. It is more important than appearance, giftedness, or skill. It will make or break a company... a church... a home. And the remarkable thing is you have a choice everyday regarding the attitude you will embrace... we are in charge of our attitudes."

SEVEN PRINCIPLES FOR ATTITUDE CONTROL

During a performance by legendary violinist, **Niccolò Paganini,** one of the four strings on his instrument snapped. The master musician stepped forward and continued playing on the remaining three strings. Soon a second string broke and finally a third. The virtuoso of the four-string did not get flustered or angry. Nor did he sulk or quit. To the delight of the stunned audience, he took another step forward and improvised his way through the remainder of the piece on the lone remaining string. When ALS tightens its grip on my life, I play on the one string it can never take from me – my choice of attitude.

Below are seven powerful principles for attitude control. Implement these principles and you will be able to play beautiful music all the way through life, even when you're down to one string.

POWER PRINCIPLE #1 - Take Complete
Responsibility for Your Attitude and Your Life

We live in an era where most everyone wants to bathe in credit when things go right, but can't point the finger of blame fast enough when they don't. Sometimes others might be to blame for troubles, but that is out of your control. What is in your control is how you respond when things go wrong. Life is at most ten percent what happens to you, and ninety percent how you react to what happens. I contracted ALS through no fault of my own. But I am one-hundred percent responsible for how I respond to living with ALS. I cannot control all circumstances of my life, but I do have control of my thoughts. That puts me squarely in charge of my attitudes and therefore my quality of life. And so it is with you.

POWER PRINCIPLE #2 - Make Peace
With What Cannot Be Changed

In high school, I heard of a young man roughly my age having been paralyzed from the waist down in a car accident. This sparked a conversation amongst my friends as to whether it would be better to live in such a condition, or better to just perish in the accident. We all preferred death. Oh, the irony. If I were paralyzed from the waist down, I would have fully functioning arms and hands. I could speak and sing clearly. I could drive a car, lift weights, play guitar, use a computer keyboard and a cell phone. I could cook my own dinner, feed myself, pop the top off my own beer and drink it myself. I could shower myself, use the toilet myself, put myself to bed, and live independently.

Imagine my current life and the lives of those around me if I could not make peace with what I cannot change. If there is a chance you can change something unpalatable in your life, then fight to change it. But if something is to be and cannot be changed, don't spend one minute or ounce of energy kicking and screaming against the inevitable. Focus your efforts where you can actually make positive change.

POWER PRINCIPLE #3 - Find the Jewel
Amidst The Rubble

The Scandinavian north wind provided bitterly cold and harsh living conditions for the Vikings. But it forced them to be tough as steel, and was the agent that enabled them to sail, travel, explore, conquer and acquire great wealth. Thus the Scandinavian Proverb: **The north wind made the Vikings**. Similarly, the two things I am most proud of- raising my daughter as a single father, and inspiring the young men in The Lake Oswego Lakers football program - could never have happened like they have if not for the harsh presence of ALS in my life. Success author Napoleon Hill wrote, "**Every adversity brings with it the seed of an equivalent advantage**." When calamity leaves our lives in shambles, search through the rubble for that jewel that becomes that seed of equivalent advantage.

POWER PRINCIPLE #4 - Immerse Yourself In A Cause Bigger Than Yourself

I have never forgotten this sentence from Dale Carnegie's fabulous work *How to Win Friends & Influence People*- **"A boil on one's neck interests one more than forty earthquakes in Africa."** I have met a lot of people that appear to get everything they want in life. Yet, I have never met a single individual that is truly happy that is consumed with Me, Myself, and I. When I began coaching football at Lake Oswego High School, I did it for my love of the game. When I saw the high character being sewn into the young men in Coach Steve Coury's incredible program, my purpose radically changed. I now see my work as part of a mission to inspire our next generation and a contribution to our collective future, a cause slightly more inspiring than the boil on my neck.

POWER PRINCIPLE #5 - Find the Good In Other People

If you cannot get along with others, you will be miserable and you will fail. Your life is shaped by relationships and interactions with others. You need the cooperation of others for achievement as well as for peace of mind. And how you see others will color the attitude you take to every interaction with them. Don't nitpick others shortcomings, look for the good in people. The great steel magnate, Andrew Carnegie, developed others so well that he had forty-three millionaires working under his tutelage. Carnegie said, **"You develop people the way you mine gold. You expect to move tons of dirt to find an ounce of gold, but you don't go in looking for the dirt – you go in looking for the gold."**

POWER PRINCIPLE #6 - Choose Interpretations of Life's Tribulations That Empower You

If life is ninety percent how you react to what happens to you, ninety percent of that is determined by your interpretation of what happens to you. When I got ALS, I confess to asking, "Why me?" But I am glad that I asked the question with a sincere desire to understand the positive reason for my suffering. My ability to counsel, motivate, and inspire others is based upon the credibility I've established for how I've responded to my suffering, as well as the insight on life it has afforded me. I could never do what I do without having gone through what I've gone through. I choose this empowering interpretation as the positive reason for my suffering.

POWER PRINCIPLE #7 - Live With An Attitude Of Gratitude

Whenever I start to feel like the deck of life has been stacked against me, I pull out and read a list I created several years ago entitled *My Life's Greatest Blessings.* I am quickly reminded of everyone and everything I have to be thankful for. Most things in our lives are right. But most of us spend our time and energy fretting over that which isn't perfect. Harold Abbott of Webb City, Missouri did exactly that until one day he met a smiling man with confidence, cheerfulness, optimism – and no legs. The man sat upon a wooden board equipped with wheels and propelled himself with a block of wood in each hand. From that day on, Abbott kept a note on his mirror that read as follows:

I had the blues because I had no shoes,
Until upon the street, I met a man who had no feet.

Even as a very young man, I instinctively understood that my choice of attitudes in life would be a life preserver or millstone around my neck. I have tried to live my life true to, and I swear by, the principles above. But if you're still unconvinced as to the importance of your choice of attitude in life, let me introduce you to someone that will be hard to argue with.

Dr. Victor Frankl was a Jewish physician held in a Nazi concentration camp during World War ll. The Nazi's killed his wife and children, took his wedding ring and everything that life meant to him. Naked and shaved, robbed of all personal dignity he stood under the glaring lights of the Gestapo. In that moment, he decided they would not destroy the one thing they could never take from him – his choice of attitude. As a result, his story of perseverance has rippled waves of inspiration throughout the world for more than seven decades. Next time you start to slip into victim mode or self-pity, don't think about my situation, remember Dr. Frankl and his decision under the lights. Life is all about choices.

Choose wisely.

ABOUT COACH JEFF

Coach Jeff Young is an inspirational writer and motivational football coach. A former college running back and rock guitarist, Jeff began having trouble holding a guitar pick in 1983. This led to an Amyotrophic Lateral Sclerosis (Lou Gehrig's Disease) diagnosis and medical prognosis of death within three to five years. Thirty-one years later, not only does he continue to befuddle medical experts, but he has also turned his tragedy into a triumphant role inspiring people the world over.

With arms, hands, and legs nearly useless, and a progressive and fatal neurological disorder hanging over his head, Jeff has spent three plus decades creatively developing ways to remain positive and optimistic. He learned just how individualistic happiness, motivation, and optimism are when he saw individuals getting everything they wanted in life and were still unhappy pessimists, while many in wretched circumstances remained cheerful optimists. He made it his mission to learn as much as he could about how to be happy, motivated, and optimistic, and to share this knowledge with as many others as possible. He began sending out *Jeff's Inspirational Quotations*, a biweekly inspirational email message of his findings and philosophy, and quickly received feedback from nearly every corner of the world in the form of praise and from those seeking advice.

Impressed with Jeff's writings, in 2004, legendary high school football coach Steve Coury asked Jeff to join his coaching staff for motivational and inspirational reasons. When both saw the incredible impact his message had on the lives of Coury's athletes, his role increased from a weekly inspirational letter to the team to include mentoring individual players and teaching leadership skills to team leaders. About Coach Jeff, Coury says, "I have been coaching for 30 years with aspirations of making a difference in young men's lives. Coach Young has a profound impact on every life he touches." After many bitter "close, but no cigar" playoff losses, in 2011, amidst tears of joy, the state championship trophy was presented to Coach Jeff in one of the great moments in Oregon high school football history.

Jeff has been featured in numerous local and national publications including Positive Thinking Magazine, and written motivational speeches for companies like Standard Insurance. He's been featured in broadcast features on ABC, CBS, NBC, FOX, Comcast Sports, CBS College Sports, and ESPN. Jeff is also part of America's PremierExperts®, a leading organization that recognizes experts from across the country. ESPN Sports Center Anchor Neil Everett recalls, "While at ESPN, I heard the story of a guy in Oregon doing remarkable things with young people on the football field. Jeff's spirit soars and his words walk for him." Despite some ominous signs of things to come for our world, Coach Jeff looks to future with the same optimism he's handled ALS with, and lives to inspire others. Jeff is a 1985 graduate of The University of Oregon and single father to daughter Priya.

Connect with Jeff at:
jeff@friendsofjeff.com
www.friendsofjeff.com
www.twitter.com/CoachJeffQuotes
www.twitter.com/CoachJeffYoung
www.facebook.com/LO48Coach
www.youtube.com/coachjeffyoung48

CHAPTER 11

GRADUATION SEASON 2014

BY MATTHEW GORDON

Let me tell you a story of a situation that happened to one of my companies this year, this is the story of Graduation Season 2014. The voices of graduation agents are increasing in volume everyday as new hires push to make themselves heard in the open floor plan office. The office itself is a hive of activity, alive with excitement, ready to burst at the seams. With each day there is a new face in a desk that wasn't there the night prior. Everyday we are expanding to accommodate the increase in orders; all departments including sales, support, web-development, marketing and production are growing. Almost as if when we leave at night and turn the lights off, the fairies of employment come in and squeeze even more desks in where we didn't think we could fit another, and leave us with a brand new employee in the morning. I find it difficult to keep up with the new names and try to remember what everyone's role is.

While we have grown every year, it seems this year the growth has a life of its own, an almost terminal velocity with its own rules. This feeling is contagious throughout the office; it's this sense of infallibility, sureness on how we got here and where we are going, and a general feeling of expected success. The dollar value of each budget is increasing along with the headcount. Each day they seem more and more bloated, and this sense of entitlement is streaming in. Yet the orders keep coming in, and the projections are getting blown away daily, so we should keep up at this pace, right? This is the way we grow, this is everything I have read about, everything we always secretly dreamed of, but never admitted that we actually wanted.

Let me tell you a little secret, this is all about to fall down. If everything you have read so far seems too good to be true, that we are growing too fast, that we need to keep expenses in line, that we should slow down on hiring, that we should be more strategic, you are right. Let me tell you why.

On an April afternoon, one of my employees is served with a multi-million dollar class action lawsuit. This is the type of lawsuit that could endanger not only the health of this company but all the related entities that I own. This is the game changer that could take everything we have done and derail it.

To make matters worse, it seems that the reporting that we have been relying on has been off and with all of those new orders, we are significantly behind on manufacturing and in a position of having to expedite materials at a much higher cost. The calls are now increasing from frustrated customers who are very unhappy that orders that they expected are now going to be delayed. The spiral continues as we realize that we have significant issues with our software – which is not allowing us to send partial orders.

Within days, the enthusiasm in the office turns into gloom. Every customer service agent takes a deep breath before answering each call, preparing for someone to scream at them. Gone are the days of hiring, gone are the days of unchecked budgets. We are in survival mode. How did we get here? How could things go overnight from living our dreams to eking out survival? This cautionary tale is one that can happen to anyone, and most successful organizations will go through something like this at some point. The real question is, did they come out the other end?

Well, before we get into what happened and how you can prevent this from happening to you, let's take a step back and let you know a bit more about us. The Gordon Group traces its origins back to the 1960's under the leadership and stewardship of my father, Carl Gordon. Our heritage of selling educational products goes back more than fifty years. Carl was a visionary in the promotional market, he grew a business out of nothing, established each relationship personally, becoming a fixture in the educational product space. Back then, graduation supplies were only a small part of the business, promotional materials and novelty items were the bigger share of our market. Carl was a marketing thought leader before we had a name for thought leaders; he introduced ideas to the world before they were prepared to accept them, and grew the business to a level of success that even he couldn't have imagined.

Unfortunately, as Carl grew older none of his children seemed particularly interested in taking over the business, except me, of course. At this time, I was a schoolteacher that always had a side business. From real estate investments, to, I kid you not, Amway; I wanted to be a business owner. So as soon as my father started discussing the legacy of the family business, I requested that he give me the opportunity. He couldn't see me leaving the comfort and stability of a teaching job for the uncertainty of business. I had to explain numerous times that I needed to grow an organization and to make my impact on the business world.

He offered the company to all of my siblings. Eventually, when no one would take him up on the offer, I approached him again and made my request. This time he grudgingly accepted and we started together in the basement of his house. That business is vastly different from the one I own today. His philosophy was one of relationships and that we should attend each and every Trade Show, as this was a handshake business. We needed to be in front of each and every person that we sold to.

I could not see this as the way to scale this business; I needed to be able to multiply my sales efforts 10x. So my first step was to stop getting on planes and traveling the world, and started putting all of my efforts into calling schools over the phone. In today's world, that idea seems so antiquated right? Well back then, my father was one of the only businesses calling international schools and pitching merchandise over the phone, at the time it was all done through Trade Shows. Was it easy? No, it was disruptive to people's ideas on how these things should be purchased. I heard no's faster and a lot more often, which allowed me to find the yes's quicker and without the travel.

The first rule I learned was, even if you find a great system you can't rely on it for long, you need to be searching for the next greatest idea. Within 1-2 years your competitors will copy you and if you have not used that head start to expand your advantage, they will find a way to take your idea and do it better, faster, or cheaper.

My next big idea came in the early 1990's when I kept reading about the Internet. When I would solicit advice from business leaders, friends and family, no one knew what the Internet was. Everyone laughed when I sank my time and money into learning html and getting my website up and running. I was one of the first 1000 sites in the world where people could buy products – at a time when thought-leaders were still discussing if email would stick around. The push on the web paid off huge, but as ideas only last for so long before your competitors are there adding something, doing it better, or finding a way to do it cheaper, we moved on to SEO. Then we changed from educational novelties and products into specialization of caps, gowns, and items that celebrate achievements.

In the 1990s, the model for educational supplies was based on the relationship between a sales rep and a school administrator. I saw the limitations of this model and the potential for selling graduation supplies over the Internet – despite industry experts emphatically telling me it would never work. But it did.

Bringing this new model to reality was a very tough road and there was no guarantee of success. It would have been so easy to give up. Our competitive advantage has been, and still is, our ability to see potential and to make it happen – despite the obstacles and even when so-called experts claim it can't be done. This is what separates us from our competitors.

This model of modernization of marketing has been our cornerstone of success. We decided a long time ago that finding opportunities in the marketplace where we could apply these new ways of reaching and engaging consumers was our model, while a particular type of product or business niche was not. That is how we started AvantiSystemsUSA. We noticed that the high-quality glass wall systems path to market was through specification books that sat in an architect's library; so our model was to make our specifications available online early and as easy to access as possible. This has been a game changer in the space, where daily we receive more inquires than we can handle.

Another important change is in the relationship between businesses and their customers -- Gen X and Gen Y don't care about the old rules of business. They want convenience, choice, speed and organisations with values they can identify with. They are always plugged in socially and share almost everything. So we have seen this change coming and have invested heavily in learning and testing new strategies on social media and emerging social platforms.

We have seen that millennials are unique, they have been brought up in a new world and they think and act differently. So we have adapted and think differently. We think that the old ways of doing things are, simply put, outdated. We are creating new playbooks and new rules to engage, accommodate, and foster the growth of our millennial workforce. So much so that we have created a number of networking, co-working, and educational groups for this millennial workforce. Without them we can have no chance at success.

Why am I telling you this? Well, because we believe that the next generation has always been and always will be what drives the engine of success. Their ideas, spirit, and efforts propel us to the next level. I have always empowered the next generation – the majority of our executive team has come up through the ranks from entry level warehouse, customer service, etc., and taken their ideas to finance, marketing, and production. So look for and train the best and brightest of the next generation. Forget looking to Harvard, look in the young entrepreneur club of your local high school. Grow your own talent, the next generation is looking for opportunities and your best path to success is to tap into this resource as early as possible.

Our challenge is to stay in front in our industry. To do that, we need to understand our customers and to be the type of company they want to be associated with.

So how did we get out of the mess we were in? Well, if I told you it was easy and there was a simple solution, I would be lying to you. I had to make some tough choices, downsize a bit, and get back to basics. It's an unfortunate reality in a growth company, but I want these organizations to be around in 40 years, not just for the next 4. What I have always relied on in good times and bad is my "Lesson Plan" or my ten things that bring me back to basics. In short, it's my cheat sheet for being a successful entrepreneur.

Fail often and early: The sooner you fail, the cheaper it is to fix your mistake. If nine out of ten businesses fail, don't you want to get your first nine failures out of the way first?

Find a way to make it possible: If anyone tells you something cannot be done, they should not be around you, find solutions-oriented people. There is always a way, you just need to find it.

Strategic Planning: Get your business on a one-page strategic plan. Be it something like Strategic Coach from Dan Sullivan or Jim Collins, find a way to get your strategy down and execute on that plan. Without it, you are just going to be a rudderless ship.

Networking for the next idea: If you want to know what the next big thing is you have to get out and find it. Join a mastermind or group that expands your thoughts. The YEC, Ryan Deiss' War Room, Yanik Silvers Maverick Group, Strategic Coach, and Infusionsoft's Elite Forum are some of my favorites.

Accommodate the way in which people work: Unless you want to compete dollar for dollar with the biggest firms, find out how your team works and work with them. Sometime a part-time remote situation can let you get an A player for 30% less than your competitor.

Know your numbers: If I didn't know my numbers and see the big picture, the events of 2014 could have caused us to cease trading. You need to find what numbers are the real heartbeats of your business and know them.

Adapt, don't be rigid (See the opportunities and don't get stuck in one mindset.): I have watched once prosperous organizations fall into success only to see the entire enterprise go bust in a few years. This is from accepting success and failing to move on to the next big idea. If you want to have long-term success keep adapting.

Live your values: We live by core values such as "Happy Happy" and "Educate, Innovate and Create." I don't want anybody to be part of the organization if they are truly not happy. If they want a different career path, all they have to do is ask. If they do not believe in the culture, we help them self-select out. Happiness is the balance that drives innovation. "Innovate, Educate, and Create" is our lifecycle of growth, how we do everything. We innovate something in the market, educate the next generation, and create something that has the ability to disrupt the market.

Start before you are ready: Have a great idea, test it today. Do it before it's ready and see just how far it can go. Stop making a product perfect; get it to market and then reform. This goes for processes as well, get it 80% of the way there; next time get it another 80%, rather than getting it perfect. Start today.

Keep Pushing: As a competitive athlete this is really the heart of my success. Every day push a little further, try a little harder; don't settle for what you achieved today. If you want to be great, you can't settle for good.

If you want to learn more: email me or check out my blog.

About Matthew

Matthew Gordon is the founder of the Gordon Group, an eclectic holding company that is focused on the modernization of marketing across industries. From educational regalia and consumer textiles to architectural products, the Gordon Group has a proven track record of disruptive innovations across industries.

A former classroom teacher and educator, Matthew was almost finished with his PHD from Columbia University when he decided to change direction and enter the business world. This career move was not made lightly as Matthew had already dedicated so much time to education, with two Masters Degrees (one in Early Childhood Education and another in School Administration) already under his belt. The choice to leave a position at a well-respected school in Greenwich, CT, where he was enjoying a growing academic career, for a business where there was no guarantee of success, was a risky one.

When Matthew joined his father's educational and novelty products company, even he didn't know that it would turn into the world's leading e-tailer of graduation caps, nor did he imagine that his gowns would be featured on the cover of Time Magazine. In those early days, the company was built upon sales generated through individual visits and interactions, much different from the e-commerce behemoth it is today. Through hard work, dedication to quality products, and superior customer service, Matthew has led GraduationSource into staggering growth year-in and year-out, with no signs of slowing down.

Matthew was not content with just one successful company and set about to turn the architectural world on its ear with the introduction of Avanti Systems in 2008. Despite searching high and low for European quality glass walls and partitions for his office, Matthew realized that the US market lacked a provider of glass products on par with what is readily available across the Atlantic. This discovery, along with some research into the antiquated way in which architectural products are specified, lead to the creation of Matthew's second largest company. Today Avanti enjoys a peerless reputation in its industry for bringing innovative and aesthetically stunning products to market.

A competitive swimmer since early childhood, Matthew can usually be found at the top of international rankings in his quest for a world record. The pool is not the only place you will find Matthew setting records on the water, he is also a power boating fanatic. Whether he is speeding through ocean waters on a record attempt or making a splash on the world stage of swimming, Matthew is always a fierce competitor. This drive permeates all aspects of his life. From the pool to the office, Matthew owes his success to consistent training and understanding that mental resilience is the key to winning any event.

To date, Matthew has been featured in *Forbes, HR.com, Brazenlife, TedX Wall Street, Startupnation, Wework, SCORE, CEO.com, Buildmybiz, Greenwich Magazine, Smart Recruiters* and numerous other publications. He has taken a number of companies from startup to the status of Inc. 500/5000 award winners, including some top 100 categories.

Always approachable and open to new ideas and inspiration, Mathew encourages thoughtful engagement via his twitter @matthewhgordon, or on his website MatthewHGordon.com.

CHAPTER 12

MANIFEST YOUR WEALTH: CREATING A LIFE OF ABUNDANCE

BY PETER LEE

As a being of Power, Intelligence, and Love,
and the lord of his own thoughts,
man holds the key to every situation,
and contains within himself that
transforming and regenerative agency
by which he may make himself what he wills.
~ James Allen

Man is the creator of his own destiny by the thoughts he chooses to consistently think. On a subconscious level, our thoughts are replaying messages of either success or failure. It is therefore the choice of man to make a conscious effort to monitor his thoughts whether they are constructive or destructive. The subconscious mind does not distinguish the difference between positive and negative ideas and thus will bring into reality one which is driven by faith just as readily as a thought driven by fear.

Quantum Physics is the study of everything that makes up the universe, which includes the physical (material world) as well as the non-physical (thoughts and feelings). Everything in the physical world is made up of molecules, which are broken down into atoms, then subdivided into sub-atomic particles, which are vibrating frequencies of energy. Anything and everything, physical and non-physical, which exists in the entire universe, when broken down is energy. So your thoughts are creative energy.

Any person with a passionate desire, precise thoughts, and faithful belief, has the ability to achieve miraculous things. Historical figures like Theodore Roosevelt, Martin Luther King, Napoleon and Alexander the Great were the genesis from which I developed an understanding of great historical leaders. Throughout my developmental years, I also studied psychology and read motivational books by Napoleon Hill, Earl Nightingale, James Allen and numerous inspirational authors. Legendary athletes like Wayne Gretzky, and Michael Jordan inspired in me the will to perform beyond expectation. These individuals may have come from different backgrounds, but they had common traits. They were fueled by a positive attitude and unshakable faith and belief to achieve the impossible. They believed in themselves and chose to create magnificence in their life.

At a very early age, I was impressed by the words of the great American President, Theodore Roosevelt. These words have inspired me and I share them with the hope they will be equally inspiring to you: "It is not the critic who counts; not the man who points out how the strong man stumbles, or where the doer of deeds could have done them better. **The credit belongs to the man who is actually in the arena, whose face is marred by dust and sweat and blood; who strives valiantly; who errs, who comes short again and again, because there is no effort without error and shortcoming; but who does actually strive to do the deeds; who knows great enthusiasms, the great devotions; who spends himself in a worthy cause; who at the best knows in the end the triumph of high achievement, and who at the worst, if he fails, at least fails while daring greatly, so that his place shall never be with those cold and timid souls who neither know victory nor defeat."**

Wealthy, successful people create their own destiny. I came to the conclusion that success starts in your mind, which evolves from your desires, driven by your belief and gratitude, and is fueled by the actions manifested by the choices you make. In this chapter I would like to share with you powerful principles that will allow you to take control of your life.

1. IMAGINATION AND VISUALIZATION OF YOUR DREAM

Dream the dream by actually defining your dream and begin to visualize it through your imagination. This is a conceptual idea, but a very necessary one. Most people only have a vague idea of their dreams. But you must create a crystal clear image of exactly what you want. Imagine it as a picture in your mind and formulate an exact description of every detail. Is it a particular home, wealth, a certain lifestyle, a specific car, a vacation destination, or a relationship? What do you desire? Once you have that defined, begin to add very identifiable details to your dream. What are the luxuries of your dream home? What color is the car you want? What will you do when you reach your vacation destination?

Your personal vision and the exacting details that make your dream uniquely yours, must be backed by a passionate desire to achieve what you intend to obtain. If you are unclear about the specific details, the universe will bring forth something you didn't want. Share your specific dreams with someone you truly trust. Make sure they are someone with whom you have an extremely close relationship and who will support and encourage you. This may be your spouse, partner or family member with whom you are building this dream. But ultimately, your dream is up to you to make it happen. Sharing your dream will make it real and this individual can provide feedback to crystallize your dream. Your well-thought-out ideas will help you create a stronger image of your dream. Keep in mind that not everyone will understand and some will tell you why it will never happen. There are plenty of "dream killers" who are negative and will discourage you by derailing you from your path.

Everyone has different dreams and different goals. You have to visualize what you want. Imagine and focus on it intently. Write it down, take pictures of it, create a dream board, talk to the appropriate people about it, and quickly you will feel the continuously growing excitement of a crystallized dream.

2. BELIEVE AS IF ACHIEVED

Pursuing a dream will inevitably bring feelings ranging from euphoria to self-doubt. These feelings are a reflection of what you believe subconsciously. Belief is a powerful element in the process to achieving your dream. When you believe you already have what you desire, you harness the creative power for fulfillment of your vision.

This is not only something that happens in your mind, but also what you feel in your body. The power of the mind is extraordinary and once you experience this level of excitement, your entire being will be vibrating with energy. Actually see it, smell it, touch it and feel it. You can see yourself owning your own business. You can see your investment portfolio growing every year. You can smell that new car smell. You can actually experience yourself living in that dream home on the property you envisioned. Feel yourself living a wealthy lifestyle. Whatever your dream is, allow yourself to feel it.

When you were a child, I'm sure you had many dreams and ambitions. Do you remember the thrill and excitement you felt? Those giddy childhood-like feelings are acceptable and in fact, they are very necessary. Grasp those feelings of your achieved dream and allow yourself to feel that excitement throughout your entire being.

This concept of "Believe as if Achieved" led me to a life-influencing experience during the global recession of 2008 which had drastically affected me financially. Everything started to collapse, my businesses stalled, my investments took losses, and I had to sell my real estate holdings. I felt negative thoughts begin to infiltrate my mind, but I made a conscious decision to stop them in their tracks and started to focus on my dreams of rebuilding my financial empire. I could have given up by blaming the economy. However, I resolved to learn from my mistakes. I visualized and believed I could rebound in only half the time. I created such a strong belief that I knew without a doubt it was going to happen. I felt gratitude with what I still had in my life during this time, which included the birth of my children. I made a commitment to rebuild what I had lost and believe that I could do it.

No matter the dream, the process is the same. If your belief system is strong enough, you will accomplish that which you set out to do!

3. ATTITUDE OF GRATITUDE

Live by a principle of gratitude. Feeling gratitude for even the smallest of things in your life is very important to what you will accomplish. Be overwhelmingly grateful for what you already have: your health, your relationships, the car you currently own, and the roof over your head.

People pray for things they need, but often they are praying from a position of lack. Their prayers are motivated by what they don't have, rather than praying out of gratitude. By focusing on what they need and don't have, they are in essence keeping themselves in an atmosphere of lack. By acknowledging in their subconscious mind that which they desire, they unknowingly focus on what they don't have rather than being grateful for what they already possess. The result is that they continue to stay where they are and fail to progress.

The proper use of prayer is to pray with deep gratitude, believing that you have received that for which you have asked. If you want a new car, give gratitude that you own it and it will come to you. You see, there is a principle continuously at work called the "Law of Attraction." That is, there are certain things we attract in our life by the way we think and act. Thoughts are energy, and like-energy attracts like-energy. If your mind is constantly focused on negative things, you will attract negative things. However, if your mind is focused on positive things, you will attract positive outcomes. As Earl Nightingale said, "Whatever we plant in our subconscious mind and nourish with repetition and emotion will one day become reality." Why does it seem that the rich get richer and the poor get poorer? It's because of their mindset.

By giving gratitude and changing your thoughts on how you view things, you will change your life completely. When you think about money do you think about not having money or the lack of money? Or do you think about having an abundance of money? If you continually think of never having enough money, you never will have enough. However, if you believe money is continuously flowing to you, you will attract an abundance of money. So you must choose your thoughts carefully, as this energy will create intentions that lead you to take actions.

4. ACTION WITHOUT DISTRACTION

While visualizing, believing, and gratitude are a part of the process, it is imperative to take planned action. By setting the first three principles firmly in place, you will attract various situations that require action. People and circumstances will start showing up in your life that will guide you. These windows of opportunity present themselves for you to seize, moving you closer to your goals.

However, if you don't act, or if you start to take action but get sidetracked by distractions in your life, your dreams will not manifest. Any actions that are not in sync with your dream can be identified as a distraction. People don't get what they want because they are derailed off course by the plethora of things that clutter their life. We often prioritize the less important things and neglect the dream we once possessed with passion. You see, if these principles are not solidly positioned, your dream isn't real enough to keep you motivated. Therefore, you must have single-mindedness toward your dream.

The most important principle is action. Without action, nothing is ever accomplished. For me, taking action was the biggest step of rebuilding my financial success after the recession. In 2009, everyone was talking about how bad the economy was and how it was going to get worse. Negative news was everywhere. This created distractions for many, obscuring the great opportunities that were about to come. I continued to follow through on my plans. After the recession, governments cut interest rates to jump-start the economy. With rates historically low, this created great opportunities in real estate and raising capital for business ventures. As an investor, I took advantage by building equity and acquired financing at the low rates. The real estate market recovery took hold and by 2011 so did the economy. Other opportunities presented themselves, as the low interest environment fuelled a surging stock market. I was in control of my life.

Be intentional in your actions and believe that it is achievable. Take the reins of your life by regaining control of your thoughts. Many people are on autopilot with self-doubt, focusing too much on the negative thoughts and news in the world. However, successful individuals realize these principles and use it to their advantage. If thoughts and everything around you are energy, you have the creative power to attract anything into your life. By utilizing your creative energy, you can manifest an abundance of wealth. The only thing we control is our mind, so direct it in such a way that it will bring your dream to fruition.

Dream your dream, feel your belief as if you already achieved it, always have an attitude of gratitude and take action without distraction. "The credit belongs to the man (or woman) who is actually in the arena, whose face is marred by dust and sweat and blood; who strives valiantly." That person is you!

Whatever the mind of man can conceive and believe, it can achieve.
~ Napoleon Hill

About Peter

Peter P. H. Lee is a business entrepreneur and investor. He began his journey in banking and investment financial accounting, which has given him extensive knowledge in financial services. With a strong interest in leveraging resources, real estate and utilizing proven techniques, he has gone on to establish several businesses and investments.

Peter is a graduate of the University of British Columbia specializing in Economics, Finance and Psychology. He currently resides in Vancouver, BC, and is a devoted husband to his beautiful wife, Cindy and loving father to his two children. He describes himself as a self-made entrepreneur inspired by the Great Ones and has created multiple successful ventures from the ground up.

Peter is also a trusted mortgage expert, and respected for his knowledge within the financial industry. He is dedicated to simplifying the process of finding creative solutions to overcome challenges in securing financing. Peter has exceptional vision in systemizing efficient strategies for his clients to maximize their opportunities in investing and purchasing of real estate. He is committed to the goal of building trust and confidence for a lifelong relationship with his clients.

His purpose is to help inspire and educate millions that to live a life of financial success, it all starts in the mind. Peter's success is centered on his philosophy that, "all things are possible when you believe."

CHAPTER 13

DEVELOPING THE LASER FOCUS AND DISCIPLINE OF A CHAMPION

BY RAZ CHAN

Learning how to focus and develop discipline are the key ingredients for achieving success in all areas of your life. Whether it is in the area of business, health, relationships, or happiness.

Many of us would like to be more focused and disciplined when working towards our goals. We wish for success, happiness, and prosperity—ultimately guiding ourselves to make lasting positive changes in our lives.

However the majority of us fail to make lasting changes. Many procrastinate by putting off our goals until the last minute, expecting great results. Many never reach their goals at all. Why is this a problem with the majority of us? Is it perhaps the pain of executing your goals requires too much work? Perhaps it's a fear of failure holding you back? For many putting off their goals is a way to play it safe. You can make yourself appear successful but in reality nothing has changed in your life. In order to make a positive impact and to be truly successful in whatever you desire, you need a system to maintain discipline and focus.

As an multiple international Brazilian Jiu-Jitsu champion and entrepreneur, I know the value of hard work, discipline, determination and focus. For those of you who do not know what Brazilian Jiu-Jitsu is, it is the martial art which revolutionized the sport fighting industry, propelling events such as the UFC into a multimillion dollar business.

Before I go into detail of how I used my martial arts background in the business world, I will talk about how I developed my system. I grew up in a poor family where money was often a topic of arguments. My father's small restaurant went bankrupt when I was at the age of 10. Even before he lost the restaurant, money was very tight around the household. I grew up learning about not having much nor expecting much. It was an unpleasant feeling to grow up seeing what kids on the other side of the tracks had.

My father was a martial arts instructor who introduced me to Taekwondo at the age of 5. My mom was very conservative and disciplined. They ran the household where it was all work and no play. All the kids were required to sacrifice leisure time to help with the family finances. However, my parents were very hard on me and it took me many years to forgive them. I learned many great things from my parents during those years of struggle. In fact, where I used to look back at my childhood experiences with contempt, I now view the experience as a gift.

Yes, my parents gave me the greatest gifts of all. Without these gifts I would have never gone on to achieve the goals I wanted in life. I succeeded where others would have failed. Those gifts were determination, focus, and discipline.

They taught me it was not okay to give up. They pushed me to always have a goal, a destination and a plan on how to get there. This was reinforced each day. Most importantly they stressed to stay committed to those goals. Being wishy-washy was not acceptable in their household.

By the time I reached adulthood, I had tons of dreams and aspirations. I wanted to attain all the things in life I didn't have as a child growing up. However, tension between myself and my parents during my childhood years brought about a negative mindset. Their desires to push me beyond my limits had consumed my everyday life. It began to burn me out by the time I reached adulthood. Instead of making steps to my goals they merely became wishes. Wishes are things I would like to achieve. However, without action, discipline and focus, they are just like the books that sit on the shelf. They are worthless if not used to its fullest.

Upon finishing university, I ended up moving thousands of miles away for a job working as an accounts payable clerk. During this time I began to question my life. Where was I going in terms of career, health, and relationships? Why was I not happy? What could I do today that will change my circumstances?

As a teen, I was not very focused or disciplined. My parents struggles with money had drained me emotionally and mentally. I began to believe my life was not going to amount to much either. Unconsciously, I carried this poor habit into my adult life. I realized in order for me to make a lasting change in my life I had to change my limiting beliefs and begin to focus on what I can do.

Then, that day at the age of 26, I decided to finally take responsibility for all aspects of my life. My health, career, self-worth, and spirituality.

As a child I was grossly underweight and often a target of bullies. Constant teasing came from kids. The most hurtful came from the mouths of my parents. When they were upset with me, they used every guilt tactic to make me feel worthless. I went through my young life never feeling I was going to be good enough.

The pain and the memories of the images spurred me on to finally take action to change. I began to hit the gym and trained rigorously. In a year I packed on almost 40 lbs of muscle.

It gave me confidence as people began to look at me differently. In turn, for the first time I started to feel good about myself. I began to love myself. This experience taught me a valuable lesson. If you focus on a painful experience, you will take determined action to remove it from your life. This painful experience will drive you, providing you with the endless fuel for long-term discipline and focus.

This lasting change helped propel me to further in my career. In 2005, I decided to start my own business after 10 years in the corporate world. There were people who didn't think I could do it who tried to talk me out of my decision. I knew in my heart, with the focus and discipline I developed from that eventful day, that where I decided to take action to make a lasting change in my life, I would be successful.

Today I am proud to say I have helped thousands of people better their lives through mind, body, and spirit. Overcoming my fears of failure allowed me to succeed in business, become an international martial arts champion, and live life according to my plan. We all have this power within us to succeed. We just need someone to help bring it out.

I would like to take this time to share with you my ten secrets for developing laser focus and discipline to health, happiness, wealth, and prosperity.

1. PICK A GOAL THAT REALLY INSPIRES YOU.

Pick one that you will think about all the time that will get you up in the morning raring to go. This can be a long-term goal or a short-term goal. If it doesn't inspire you, then you will have to find another goal. Find something you are passionate about. It could be to be the top sales person in your department in six months time. Perhaps it could be to prepare a plan to develop profitable new markets for your business within a year.

They could be time-management goals. For instance, perhaps you are a chronic procrastinator. You realized this problem has caused you to underperform in life. You decided today you want to change that by focusing on how to eliminate this problem.

2. WRITE DOWN ALL YOUR GOALS BOTH SHORT TERM AND LONG TERM.

Writing down you goals gives you something tangible to refer to. It serves as a constant reminder on why we do what we do. I believe many of us do not do this enough or not at all. By not doing this we are going through life directionless. It's like trying to navigate through a dense forest without a compass. Where is your destination? How are you going to get there? By what day or what time?

Unless you do this you will not find success in any part of your life.

3. ADD A DATE TO THE GOALS AND WHEN YOU WOULD LIKE TO ACCOMPLISH THEM.

I get very excited when I do this. It makes the goal feel as if it were already achieved. Once again having a date lets me gauge how close I am to reaching the milestone. By doing this you can begin to take small steps each day towards that goal.

4. VISUALIZE ACCOMPLISHING THE GOAL.

Think of the pleasurable feelings it will give you to accomplish them. Visualization is a big factor when it comes to achieving success. It is used by all successful people in life.

There was actually a study done one time on two basketball teams. One team shot free throws without visualization, while the other team practiced free throws but imagined themselves successfully hitting their shots over and over again. The study concluded the team who used visualization outperformed the team that didn't use it.

5. USE PHYSICAL IMAGES.

Place a photo beside the goal you want to achieve. For example, if it's more money you desire, get a photo of a bunch of $100 bills stacked together.

What does it mean to you? How does it feel? Act as if you have already accomplished this goal.

6. TAKE MASSIVE DETERMINED ACTION TO ACHIEVE YOUR GOAL.

At first the small steps may not seem like much but you have to look at it as a cumulative effort. It's like a tsunami, when it starts off the wave is small, but as it gathers momentum and reaches the shore, it's at full power.

This is no different when working towards your goals. It doesn't matter if it's for health, business, happiness, wealth or success in life. Keep working a little bit each day and you will get there in the end.

7. CELEBRATE YOUR SUCCESSES ALONG THE WAY TO ACHIEVING YOUR GOAL.

It doesn't matter how small you may think it may be. Take time to reward yourself. Quite often we worry about whether or not we are making progress towards our goal. We constantly wage that battle in our heads where one voice tells us we can't do something.

By celebrating a small success, you re-affirm the belief that you are well on your way to your goal. The celebration doesn't have to be grand. Just acknowledge it. I like to write down my successes every night before I go to bed. I keep a journal on my daily successes. I prefer to write at least three successes for the day. Don't sweat it if you don't have three, sometimes you will only have one.

Keep it simple. An example of a small daily success could be reading a book that has helped you overcome your fear of selling. The possibilities are endless, so be creative and open up your mind. This is for you. No one is going to judge you!

8. STAY FOCUSED DESPITE SETBACKS.

Many people abandon their goals and never reach them. The reason is because they don't believe they can attain them, or they fear success or fear failure. Another reason is that they run into an obstacle along the way. There will be many instances where this will happen. The one thing you must ask yourself is: What is the cost if I don't reach my goal? Will I lose my job, lose the big sale, or lose the respect of my team.

9. STAY COMMITTED TO YOUR GOALS BUT BE PREPARED TO IMPROVISE.

If things are not working the way you like it's okay to try another tactic. Always have an alternate route to your goal. However, keep marching towards your goal. Don't give up so easily.

10. BE PERSISTENT.

Never accept "No" or "I can't" as a reason for stopping. All champions are persistent and focused on their end goal. They never abandon their ultimate destiny. Think of all the great champions who overcame obstacles, champions like Muhammad Ali or Michael Jordan. I was repeatedly told I would never make it as a martial artist and I ended up going on to win multiple international championships.

If I can do it, so can you!

About Raz

Raz Chan has helped thousands of clients overcome their limitations to achieve success in life. His passion for helping others discover their inner greatness can be traced to his challenging childhood. During this period, he struggled with racism, poverty, low self-image, and trying to find his identity. His immigrant parents struggled to make a day to day living. The one thing they did have was a dream for a better life. Times were tough, sacrifices were made by the family. It is during this time he learned the value of hard work, determination, and tenacity.

After completing his studies he moved to Vancouver, BC. Still struggling with his negative childhood experiences, he began to re-examine his life. He sat in his little apartment one day, staring at the mirror, realizing that was not him and he wanted better. He decided a change had to be made on a physical level if he wanted to start loving himself. He began a daily intense physical regimen to transform his body by adding 40 lbs of muscle.

Along the way, he noticed the physical changes still weren't enough to bring him satisfaction. Something was missing. He was still unhappy, unfilled, and not financially successful – despite working in a white collar job. He realized his negative childhood experiences were leading him down the path to failure. Instead of living his life by design, he was living it by default.

He began to read books on self-development. Suddenly changes began to take place. He felt empowered to regain control of his life and change it for the better. In 2005, he took a chance leaving his secure government job to start Raz Chan Fitness (www.razchanfitness.com) offering the world's first women's kickboxing boot camp. It was an instant success and transformed the lives of thousands of women through health and wellness in the Vancouver area.

Today Raz has expanded his services to a worldwide audience, providing self-improvement through health and wellness through his website: www.razchan.com.

Raz was also recognized for his heroism in August 2014 when he helped stop an attempted carjacking and assault in Vancouver.

Raz is a graduate of the University of Manitoba and holds a diploma in manual osteopathy. He is an international Brazilian Jiu-Jitsu champion holding titles as a two-time US Open Champion and a two-time World Silver Medalist. His work has been featured and quoted in *The New York Times*, Canada's *Fashion* Magazine, *The Fight Network* and *Vancouver Magazine*. You can connect with Raz at:

Raz Chan Online:
raz@razchan.com
www.razchan.com
www.facebook.com/razchaninc
www.twitter.com/razchan

Raz Chan Vancouver Classes:
raz@razchanfitness.com
www.razchanfitness.com
www.facebook.com/razchanfitness
www.twitter.com/razchanfitness

CHAPTER 14

LEARN, SET GOALS AND TAKE ACTION

BY DANIEL HAMILTON

I grew up on a 162 acre turkey farm in Central Ohio. It was a very small town where few people seldom ever left. Growing up, I never knew what I wanted to do but I was very clear on what I did not want to do. What intrigued me the most was the people around me and why the world was the way it was. However, what did not interest me was to follow the same path as everyone else. I loved to play sports, travel, and share experiences with friends around me. I know what some of you are thinking.... Well don't we all? But there is the thought in your head saying you need to grow up, and face it, we will all have to work a job and forget what we want, so we can survive and give ourselves and our families our needs. Well, fortunately, through some initial ups and downs I have been able to create a "working" lifestyle that fits my childhood dreams. I have traveled to over 20 countries, owned multiple luxury cars, invested and owned multiple businesses – with my main business being able to provide me a steady growing residual income, and also allowing me the time to enjoy life and wake up when I want to. I am here to share with you some of the lessons I have learned so far.

I believe success is determined by your I.Q. What do you mean, my I.Q?? You might question....

Yes, your I.Q., and I do not mean a test where you get a score that determines whether you are in the idiot or genius percentile, I am talking about your I.Q. level = your I QUIT level.

Let me describe it in a diagram for you:

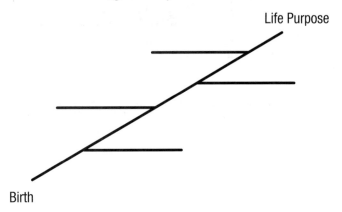

I believe we are all born with a purpose. Our purpose gives us fulfillment and happiness. But I believe it is a lifelong journey of overcoming challenges. So imagine each challenge like a test on the diagram. When we fail this particular test, we fall off the line, then we must work, travel and grow to get back onto our path towards our life purpose. Here is the tricky part that very few account for, which is, that same test is going to come back in a different form before the universe will let us move on to the next step in our life. This is where I see many people get stuck and never accomplish their life's purpose or ever live a truly fulfilling life. Allow me to give you a few stories to let this sink in.

I had a friend we will call him John. He was dating this girl who was the total opposite of him. She was quiet around his friends and awkward with his family, never worked a job and assumed he would support her. One day he realized, "WOW! I am not happy in this relationship so I need to move on," and he ended the relationship. Then a few months later, I got a call from John and he was VERY excited and remarked, "I met this girl. I think she is great, you have to meet her." So we all went to dinner and she was very quiet at the dinner and oddly looked very similar to his previous girlfriend. Then, as time went on, I started getting the complaints! "Man she is very awkward around my family, she just quit her job, she thinks I am going to pay all the bills, etc." HAHA! So I think you can see where I am going with this one… John's life would not move forward because as he was moving forward he was not overcoming his tests. Not only this, but also in his job he was in the same place financially as well as in his personal health and fitness. He was what we could call S-T-U-C-K! As I get to meet more people in my life, I find more and more people who are STUCK. Some are STUCK due to poor relationships, complacency, inconsistent work ethic, personal doubt, and even with addictions to sex, drugs or alcohol.

So how can we ensure we do not get STUCK? How can we become aware of challenges that are testing us and make sure we don't get STUCK? I do believe most people are unaware they are being tested, so inevitably, if unaware they are failing, they begin to QUIT on a life way below their purpose, and once we have QUIT on this hope of a better life, we get further and further from fulfilling our purpose. So I cannot help anyone to remove their challenges or their tests, but I can help prepare you to raise your IQ and continue to overcome so we can reach a fulfilled life.

ACTIONS THAT LOWER YOUR IQ

Comparison

As humans we all compare. The moment we walk into a restaurant and everyone is in a suit and we are wearing jeans, we begin to feel uncomfortable and perhaps want to leave the restaurant. Other examples can be when a friend or co-worker gets a raise and we do not. Or when a teammate has a great game and we played poorly. Or when a classmate seems to effortlessly get an A and we seem to always be struggling. I have found when we compare, we are setting a ceiling for ourselves and by doing this we will always be just behind. Look at it as driving a car down the Interstate. If your eyes are so fixed on the car in front of you, You will never be able to pass that car. So how do we raise our eyes off the people we are comparing ourselves to? Here are some things that have worked for me:

Action plan:

1. I repeat to myself in my head, "Do your best, be your best."

2. When there are obstacles, I repeat to myself, "Small thing to a giant."

3. I repeat these phrases in my head to keep me focused down the road and on the BIG picture.

Overthinking

You can learn a lot from race car drivers. Most accidents on the track come when the racers get out of the moment and they begin to think. The moment they think instead of intuitively reacting, they turn or hit the brake that begins a chain reaction of cars piling up. Thinking back to our diagram, it is a progressive line upwards. When we stop to overthink, we are looking from side to side, there is no action moving forward, and our IQ gradually gets lower and lower. This is because we are losing the momentum of action in our life. Now let's not take this as a need to be reckless and never think or plan. Clear, progressive planning and strategizing can be very effective and help with ultimate efficiency. However, once a plan is made, it is time for immediate action and implementation. The overthinker continues to second guess and worry to the point he/she will never know if their plan would really work – because it was never executed. This is known as analysis-paralysis.

Action plan :

1. Use a planner to calculate activities that give results – such as in sales calls, doing presentations, and following up on prospective clients. Overthinking examples are: re-doing the PowerPoint, re-doing the sales script, or re-doing the follow up Excel to perfection. *Fill your time with action that gives you results.*

2. Surround yourself with action-oriented people. (We will touch more on that later.)

Holding onto negative relationships

Some people believe that they are doomed by their relationships. They think, "Because it is family, what am I supposed to do?" or "They have been my "best friend" for so many years I have to be there for them." To me the answer is simple. Your relationships that you value, YOU choose. How you go about choosing them will create everything for you. There are many people that I have had to let go, so I could move up in my life. Now here is the great thing once you have grown. You might be able to help raise these people up as well, but only if they are willing.

Action plan :

1. List your friends and family you speak with, and honestly assess if they inspire you towards your purpose or if they deter you.

2. Increase contact with those that inspire and decrease contact with those that deter you.

3. When you remove them, don't let them creep back into your mind. I personally remove them from social media, remove old pictures, and any old activities that remind me of the person. When you empty your cup of dirty water, you allow clean water to come back in!

ACTIONS THAT INCREASE YOUR IQ

1. *Knowing your goals*
For the last 6 years, my wife and I have made a special day out of writing and reviewing our goals to start the year. We also do a quarterly review to keep us on track. We set goals based on Finance, Relationship, and Personal goals. I can tell you this is the single most important thing in our relationship and our success. Having a clear goal with an ideal action plan has done miracles in our life.

2. *Taking Action*
I believe this is the single most important thing for you to ACCOMPLISH your purpose. The mind is progressive when in action. The mind will always find ways to improve, grow and be more efficient when taking action to achieve your goals. Think about the last activity you carried out taking action towards your goals – how did you feel? I think for most of us, we felt great because there is no fear, self-doubt, comparison, or overthinking when we are totally taking

action towards our goals. The other day I sent out a text to someone I work with that just said, "Make a sales call!" and they responded "I am in the bathroom." So I responded, "Make a sales call!" So they did...It wasn't even 15 minutes after that I got a call from the person and they said, "Wow! I was having a slow day but that one call reminded me of ten people I have been meaning to call. So I called them all, and six agreed to buy." I asked, "How do you feel now?" They said "Great!" ...and I responded "Let's remember this feeling, because next time we feel slow or down, all we need to do is begin taking action towards our goals to completely change our mindset for where we are heading."

3. *Celebrating personal victories*
Along the way you will achieve many small victories. Don't EVER overlook these things as insignificant - CELEBRATE! Life is amazing when we are on a great journey of discovering and living our purpose – celebrate each step.

4. *Create a positive environment*
I believe your support system is crucial for lifting your IQ. You want to create an environment that inspires you towards your purpose. Your environment consists of your friends, family, home, work, and lifestyle. For most of us along the way, one or all of these areas aren't perfect, which is ok, but we can always be working to influence change to make improvements in each area. This will continue to lift us up along our road of overcoming challenges.

5. *Identifying and overcoming challenges*

Years ago in my first business, I reached a comfortable level of success and remember thinking that I had it "all figured out. With this one thought began my demise, and I started losing some business. As my business started to decline, I did not change. I believed it would all come back because I had it "all figured out," and after two years I was left with debt and sorrow. Then after six more months I had to be honest with myself. I had fallen far off the line that led toward my life purpose, and when faced with more challenges, I kept falling into the same pattern and life became worse and worse! My I.Q. had nearly been broken. I was close to quitting and settling for an unfulfilled life.

I realized that my challenge was letting myself be convinced I had it "all figured out." ...And I needed to re-apply myself.

It took me several years of work to recover and get back on track, and when business started to boom again I got the same feeling – I felt I had it "all figured out" (remember life will always re-test you before it lets you move on toward your life purpose). WOW! I remembered again as I identified my ego that had caused years of financial pain and suffering, and as I overcame this to change my mindset that I had to keep learning, taking action, and setting goals, my life has now risen to a level that I never thought possible. So sometimes identifying and overcoming challenges are personally hard, as we are in a fight with our ego, but once we have identified and moved on it – it is like a burden being lifted off our back.

SUMMARY

In summary, I want to thank each of you for stopping by this chapter to have a quick read. Some of these points are very summarized, and I do intend in elaborating on these points and many more of the lessons I have learned so far in my journey in future books and videos. My greatest hope is that something I have said here will spark someone out there to increase their I.Q., keep taking the steps to overcome challenges and moving one step closer to accomplish their life purpose.

About Daniel

Daniel Hamilton has had a passion for entrepreneurship, leadership, and international business from a young age. In 2001, due to a chronic digestive problem called Crohn's disease, Daniel's college football dreams were cut short when he collapsed due to heat exhaustion and almost lost his life. Growing up in a small farm town in Ohio, Daniel's father always shared with him that while the farm work may be dirty and the hours may be long, working for yourself and no one else was the true path to happiness. You should be able to live the life you want to live, instead of the life you have to live. This was a philosophy that Daniel adopted and remembered through every failure, growth and eventual success.

From there, Daniel realized he needed to take a different path, and under the mentorship of several business leaders, he opened his first company in technology sales where he began doing sales and development training in several cities in the Midwest, and eventually different countries around the world. This experience enabled Daniel to understand the struggles and hardships of being an entrepreneur and what it takes to become successful at a young age.

Moving to New York City in search of more opportunities, Daniel was met with more challenges than he anticipated. Being forced to work multiple jobs at odd hours, his health rapidly declined, even putting him at 30 lbs under his ideal weight. Luckily, Dan met his future wife Cindy, who would eventually impact his life tremendously forever. Daniel was introduced to a company called YorHealth, which focuses primarily on digestive health and balance, which would spark a rapid change in his life. As his health gradually improved, he realized that his mission was to share his story and help the company impact many others looking to change their own lives as well.

Using his previous experiences and strong philosophy, Daniel has helped grow YorHealth into a multi-million dollar enterprise, sharing with thousands of individuals the power of creating self-change and becoming un-stuck in your life. Today, YorHealth has been ranked as the fastest growing Health and Nutrition Company by the DSA in 2012. It has also been recognized by the INC 5000 as one of the fastest growing companies in America for 3 years in a row. Along with his wife, Cindy, they have together grown to be one of the top earners in the company, and are dedicated to help the organization surpass the billion dollar mark.

Daniel has a passion for educating people on possibilities. He believes that not everyone is meant to be an entrepreneur, but he also believes that it's critically important that they are given the education to know anything is possible. He believes fulfilling your purpose must be greater than just surviving.

When not traveling or working on his passions, Daniel is very active in Basketball and Australian Rules Football. His local Aussie Rules football team won Division 2 National Championship last year as part of the USAFL. Daniel and his wife enjoy the company of their English bulldogs Scarlett and Grey, and passionately root for their favorite teams – the Ohio State Buckeyes and the Cleveland Browns.

CHAPTER 15

THE POWER OF GRATITUDE

BY SPENCER McDONALD

HOW A BEGGAR TAUGHT ME THE UNSHAKABLE FOUNDATION FOR SUCCESS

A number of years ago, I met a man who changed my life. He taught me the single most important lesson I ever learned about wealth, life and success. He did it in about 3 minutes, and he didn't intend to. Now I want to share it with you.

At the time, I was a young man and my first attempt at business had failed. I was deeply in debt and I felt pretty sorry for myself. I had big ideas when I started the business, but as it went slowly under and I finally had to admit that it would not succeed, I went into a deep depression.

I registered for social assistance, and humiliated, received my first welfare check. Soon after, I was walking near the local park and I saw two men sitting on the curb outside the local store. One of them looked up and asked for spare change. "We are trying to get enough together for a six-pack." he said.

I don't know why I stopped. Usually, I walk right past panhandlers without making eye contact but today I stopped. Perhaps it was the direct and honest way that he asked for beer money, or it might have been his smile. I don't know, but I stopped.

They were dirty. I mean really dirty, like they had been sleeping on the ground. Their hair was matted and filthy and their clothes smelled bad. I said to him "How are you doing today?" and he replied "Great! It's a great day, how are you?" I was depressed and feeling sorry for myself, but there was no way that I would tell this street person my problems. I said, "Okay."

"Don't you love the spring?" he continued. "We live outside. I just love when it warms up a bit." He smiled broadly, "We have a great place in the middle of the park. Nobody else knows about it and we don't get bothered. It's dry too! It's inside a stump." He whispered like he was letting me in on a secret.

Now, this is possible. The park is a huge forest; part of the university endowment lands and filled with massive stumps from the old growth timber cut many years ago. Some were ten or more feet across and have a tendency to rot out from the inside, leaving a fairly big space there. As a kid, I built forts in stumps like that.

Now that he was talking, he just kept going. "We have everything we need," he said enthusiastically. "We stop by the church mission for dinner and find lots of good stuff in the garbage. You wouldn't believe what folks throw out! There are a couple of restaurants where they scrape a few plates into those little take home containers and leave them on top of the dumpster so we don't have to dig for them. It's just great." He smiled, "People are so kind."

I didn't know what to say. I had been feeling sorry for myself but I still had a car, an apartment, clean clothes and food. This guy had nothing compared to me, yet he seemed happy and felt lucky. He was having a good day!

I felt ashamed of myself for daring to feel bad about my situation when someone with far less than I could be happy and still have so little. I pulled out a $5 bill and handed it to him. He reached out slowly to take it and wide-eyed, turned to his friend saying, "Look at this, five bucks!"

I walked away as they were headed into the store holding up the bill and smiling. I suddenly had mixed feelings and thought about whether

I had done the right thing. I thought I should have never given them money; they are just going to waste it! I felt ripped off, somehow fooled or manipulated into feeling guilty and giving up the bill. Then I started feeling guilty about being angry, and then angry with myself for even stopping.

"This is nuts" I said.

As I calmed down, I decided to try and figure out my feelings about it. It seemed important to understand what had just happened. Somehow the whole thing was significant but I wasn't getting it.

As I replayed the exchange in my mind, I recalled one statement that he had made, the one that seemed the most outrageous. "We have everything that we need," he said as he expressed an immense sense of gratitude for everything positive in his situation. I tried to put myself in his place and imagine living in a stump, eating other people's leftovers for lunch, panhandling for beer money and thinking that it was enough. It was tough. I had never gone hungry. I had always had a roof over my head. Ever since I was old enough to drive, I had owned a car.

But I was deeply depressed, resentful and unhappy. I asked myself, "What would make me happy?" That's easy I thought: To be rich instead of broke. I would be happy if I had the things that I wanted in life...when I had all the money to buy whatever I wanted.

How much was that? A million dollars? Ten million? A billion?

I was stumped. Every time I imagined what I wanted, I kept adding more to the list. There were bigger houses, faster cars, longer vacations, fatter bank accounts, fancier boats, flashier girlfriends, even airplanes! I tried to put a dollar amount on it but I couldn't seem to find a reasonable expectation. This went on for days and then weeks.

The question burned in my mind: "How much is enough?"

The words of the panhandler kept coming back: "We have everything we need."

Finally, I got it. When there seems to be no answer to your question, perhaps the question itself is at fault. I had been asking how much is enough to make me feel rich and be happy and content. I suddenly realized that I had been asking the wrong question!

So I asked myself "What do I need? What do I need to live? What are the basics?" In a flash I realized that I already had everything that I needed. I already had a home, a way to get around, food, good friends, family that loved me. And I even had enough to give the beggar five bucks out of my wallet for beer.

I had more than enough!

I just couldn't see it through the fog of my resentment over what I DIDN'T have.

I knew that I really did have more than enough of everything that I needed including money, even though I still had much less than what I wanted. This changed my perspective on money and wealth, and I began to have gratitude for having so much more than my basic needs.

That was the moment in my life where I began to understand and achieve success.

What I learned from the panhandler is that wealth is really all in your mind. It's relative and it changes, not only from person to person, but over time in the same person. In the moment that we met, he was the wealthier and I was impoverished even though I had more money, because that is how we both saw ourselves. That was the reality that we had both constructed for ourselves to live in.

In a nutshell, I was already wealthy, I just didn't believe it, and so I couldn't see it! We create reality with our thoughts, feelings, beliefs and actions. Living in a mindset of lack and impoverishment does not attract wealth or generate motivation and energy for positive action.

If you are obsessed as I was, with the LACK of money or success, your reality is all about lack, need, want, impoverishment and desperation about it all. You may even have good reasons to blame others for your situation. That does not attract wealth or generate enthusiasm to get out and create something. Negative thinking and blaming attitudes suck the energy out and disempower you. The path to success, greatness and true wealth begins with recognition and gratitude that most or all of our needs are fulfilled right now.

Having gratitude for what you have now is different from being satisfied or complacent. On the contrary, the most successful, driven entrepreneurs with the greatest yet-to-be-realized goals are far from complacent or satisfied. They are driven to succeed and work hard to achieve their goals, but they do it from a place of abundance and gratitude – not fear and resentment.

You must become wealthy and successful in your mind first. From an attitude and reality of abundance, setting goals and reaching for more will satisfy a desire to challenge yourself to have more, do more and experience more than you do now. The joy is in both the journey and achievement of the goal!

Just as I was when I met the panhandler, you may be focused on what you don't have, or the bills that you have to pay, or other things that are wrong in your life and how unhappy you are about your situation. Gratitude is the unstoppable force that changes this reality.

For at least 10 minutes or more every day, focus on what you are grateful for. If you have problems doing this, look around you and notice the people who have so much less. Do this out loud or write it down in a journal. If you have spiritual beliefs, thank and express gratitude to God, but the important thing is to express gratitude. What are you grateful for? Do it every day. And do it out loud. Then, throughout your day, look for and notice everything that you have to be grateful for, and express that gratitude.

Your gratitude will probably include your family, the fact that you have a warm bed and a roof to sleep under. My list includes gratitude for my health and talents, family, friends and even my pets. Include the weather, the way your garden looks, the person who let you into traffic; everything that you can think of and say it out loud. Got that, say it out loud! Speaking it makes it much more powerful. Look for the good in everything and everyone and express gratitude.

Commit to doing only this one thing and it will change your life.

Understand that you are not being grateful for being satisfied or for having everything that you want. You will never have everything that you want and you will keep setting new goals to strive for. You are getting really clear that in fact you have MORE than what you need right now, and you are expressing gratitude for that and everything else good in your life.

You are changing the focus of your thinking. You are learning to think like successful wealthy people think and it's this thinking that drives your reality and will propel you to massive success!

Now, set your goals and write them down. Build a treasure map with pictures and do it all from a reality of gratitude, wealth and abundance instead of lack, fear and impoverishment. You will see spectacular results.

There are many skills and techniques that you can learn from this book to become ultra-successful and wealthy but the very first step is gratitude. Although I watched for him, I never saw my panhandler/teacher again. I will never forget him though and I'm grateful to this day for the lesson that he taught me without knowing it or intending to—the most important lesson of my life.

Find gratitude for what you have now. Then see and feel yourself successful and wealthy and believe it. It is then only a matter of space, time and hard work to bring your goals into reality.

Start now: **What are you grateful for?**

About Spencer

Spencer McDonald is a nationally recognized, award-winning author and business professional who has appeared on television, radio and stages across North America. He is the Founder and President of Spencer McDonald & Associates Inc. and Thinking Driver, an international company that provides training and consulting on vehicle safety to government and industry.

Spencer rose from humble roots as an adopted child in a middle class family to become a leader in his field. He was awarded the 2008 Transport Canada Award of Achievement and the 2013 Canadian Society of Safety Engineering Award of Achievement.

He is a respected and frequently-published author and has written extensively for Canadian and U.S. publications. Having built a successful international training business, Spencer is giving back by sharing his four decades of business experience with fellow entrepreneurs, and business leaders.

Spencer draws on the challenges he overcame as a survivor of abuse and bullying as a child and subsequent episodes of depression as an adult, as well as the day-to-day hurdles he faced and surmounted, to become a successful entrepreneur delivering presentations that move and motivate with a focus on value-added, actionable, takeaway concepts.

An adventurer and motorsport enthusiast, Spencer is a Canadian motorcycle racing National Champion and extreme adventure motorcyclist. He has ridden motorcycles from Death Valley to the Arctic Circle. He is also a nationally certified sailing instructor and has skippered and taught in the waters of the U.S. and Canadian west coast and in the Caribbean. His expertise as a master trainer led him to be called on by the Justice Institute to train emergency vehicle operators, including police officers, in advanced and pursuit driving.

"I always seem to end up teaching what I love to do, that's why I ended up teaching people to drive almost any vehicle including police cars, to ride motorcycles and to sail. That is also why I am so passionate about teaching people how to achieve greater success as an entrepreneur or within a corporate structure."

As a sought-after keynote speaker, he has delivered a multitude of speeches and trainings across North America focused on his principal message, "You create your reality." Dr. Dawn Howard-Rose, PhD in Educational Psychology says: "Spencer isn't just a skilled facilitator, he wrote the book on group facilitation."

Spencer McDonald inspires, entertains, teaches, trains and motivates audiences to be more, do more, achieve more and have more. He is a Certified Master Trainer and communicator with certifications in Counselling and Hypnotherapy.

Spencer is not just a speaker or motivator: he is an entertaining keynote speaker with a message. He brings "boots-on-the-ground" experience in achieving business success in challenging economic times, both inside and outside of corporate environments.

Reach Spencer at:
smcdonald@thinkingdriver.com
1-877-250-5601
www.SpencerMcDonald.com

CHAPTER 16

HOW TO DEVELOP YOUR PERSONAL STRATEGIC PLAN

BY SHAWN ONEILL

Inaction breeds doubt and fear. Action breeds confidence and courage. If you want to conquer fear, do not sit home and think about it. Go out and get busy.
~ Dale Carnegie

And get busy I did. I thought I had a plan: work hard, be dependable, and be confident. But as you are going to learn, this was not a personal strategic plan.

Here was my idea of a plan: Get out of college fast, land a "great" job, climb the corporate ladder, live this awesome life with a house in the city, a beach house, buy a boat to hang out with friends and of course, retire early. I didn't know what exactly I was going to do, but I was going to retire while I was young, that was a definite.

So my "plan" started off well – graduating with an accounting degree in four years from a prestigious university with a solid reputation. Not bad, my plan was going well considering many people take five years to complete the degree I earned. Mark the first item off of my list... done!

I then had two paid internships at big name companies that led to my "great" corporate job. My plan was in full force. This first position was with an Internet start-up – the pay wasn't impressive but it offered plenty of potentially valuable stock options.

During this time I watched three life-changing events.

(1). The Internet boom

(2). Other people getting rich, and...

(3). The dot.com bust

The Internet boom, and *Other people getting rich:* A small startup company, half.com, located in the same building that I worked in was sold to eBay for roughly $350 million. Other "kids" fresh out of college in the same position as myself were worth a million or more. Can you believe this was happening in a suburb of Philadelphia? How wild. The next one was a company right down the street. Buy.com. The owner sold his interests for $195 million right before the company went public. At the time, Buy.com was huge; they had just broken Compaq's first year record for sales. The Internet boom was in full throttle.

I didn't really understand our company's strategy, but we were a huge online auction site for dental and medical equipment. We thought there was an opportunity to be bought out by eBay. Sales were stacking up and our online traffic was climbing by the day. We didn't even care about profit, I don't think I ever heard it mentioned. It was all about website traffic—how many visitors, and how many new registrants there were on the site. It seemed like any day we might be bought out. So my plan, it seemed, to retire early and have a great beach house, was right on track – that is, until the middle of March 2000.

The Bust: The market was very volatile. Within the next few months it was apparent that we weren't going to get bought out, and like many companies at that time, we ran through money until we went out of business. I did receive some severance pay. I thought that was great. I would have the summer off, a nice break from all of my hard work from college. But, I realized, for others unemployment was a very different experience. It especially made me feel for those with families depending upon them. They were going to have to sell a car, take the kids out of private school, even sell their dream home just to move to whatever city they could find another job. It was a crazy time.

But I landed on my feet. My plan was not going to be deterred. I acquired a job as a computer consultant, a business process analyst to be exact, before the summer was over. They sent me to a two-month training program outside of Chicago with some other really smart people from across the country. When I came back from training, I landed on a project team for a Fortune 50 company.

But the economy was shifting again. I saw the industry cut in half. When my mentor was packing up his desk, because he was laid off, it changed my view of climbing the corporate ladder. Paul must have been making a six-figure-plus income, a big office, a pension plan, and a company car allowance. He was so close to where I thought my plan would take me. I couldn't believe it. But I thought: surely he will land on his feet and find a great job.

He was incredibly smart, had an MBA, and clients loved him. When I went to talk to him about what his plans were, he was sobbing quite loudly. I went over to console him. But he was angry, "How could they do this to me?" "I have two kids coming up on college. We are going to have to sell the house, maybe the cars. I don't know what I'm going to do. No one is going to hire a middle-aged man like me, not unless it's at a very big discount."

At this point he said something that changed the course of my life.

"Shawn, business is changing. You can't count on any company to take care of you; you have to do it yourself." It was at that moment that I committed. I committed to start my own business. It was going to be sooner and not later. I did not want to end up like Paul. I knew my plan was going to have to change.

So this crazy twenty-six year old, fresh off the dot.com bust and recession, propelled by the events of 9/11 and the experience with his mentor, got his real estate license. I was determined after dabbling in the real estate market in the Philadelphia area for about a year to start a business.

I wrote up a "business plan" (really just a profit and loss budget), I shopped it at a few banks. They all turned me down of course. After vetting it with my family, they somehow allowed me to take out the equity in my home and start a business. My plan was working, I already had bought the house in the city I wanted and a nice new car, and now I was going to start a business.

Now none of this was not strategic, as Dale Carnegie said, *Action breeds confidence and courage.* If you want to conquer fear, do not sit at home and think about it. What was really crazy was that I started this business in Florida. I told you I was a crazy twenty-six year old. While I was selling homes, and running a business, I found my God-given talent: a desire to help others achieve their goals.

I made a commitment to help each of the six agents that signed on to start this brand new real estate company—beat their best year in sales. We were successful in achieving the mission. By helping each of those agents be successful, I became successful. Over the next few years we grew that tiny, independent company to one of the top real estate companies in the area.

For five years, I worked very hard growing people to high levels of success, despite my inexperience in the real estate business. My plan was working, I had a great life. But I didn't have a strategic plan...let alone an exit plan. So when the market began to shift, even though I had companies attempting to buy me out and millions of dollars were being offered...I missed out on a golden opportunity.

In trying to please everyone else, and not having a strategic vision and plan for the business, I missed out...

> *I don't know the key to success, but the key to failure is trying to please everybody.*
> ~ Bill Cosby

I was successful in creating a business that created more money and freedom than I could have dreamed of in my 20's, but I failed because I did not have a written, strategic vision and plan. I lost millions of dollars, created financial stress on my family and then missed the opportunity to be set up financially for life. **I want to help you to avoid the pitfalls and mistakes I made.** I want to share with you the 8 steps to creating a personal strategic plan. Designing the 'life wants' includes a strategic plan for each facet of your life. These steps can be applied to your Spiritual, Family, Emotional, Financial, Career, Physical and Social Goals.

If could design the perfect day, what would it look like? How about the perfect year? What about the perfect life? That was the ultimate question I asked myself.

8 STEPS TO ACHIEVE YOUR GOAL THROUGH A PERSONAL STRATEGIC PLAN.

Creating Your Strategic Plan

In this process, you learn the exact method that we used to build Jacksonville Expert Home Advisors (JEHA), the business that will allow me and those around me to truly live a life with intent. JEHA creates the time and money to achieve my career and financial goals.

It all starts with your "Why" – The purpose, cause, or belief that inspires you to do what you do.

Step 1: Create a personal Vision statement — Where do I want to be in 10 years?

– What is my BHAG (Big Hairy Audacious Goal)
  For example: I want to have the time and money to create magical memories with my family and loved ones.

– Ask yourself these 3 questions:

   a. How do I want to be remembered?

   b. What is important to me?

   c. What do I want?

For example:

   a. I want my family to remember me as loving, fun, and available for them no matter what.

   b. Loved ones, and living life on a schedule of my choosing.

   c. Create enough leveraged capital that I can live life by design with freedom and autonomy.

Step 2: Create a personal mission statement — How do you envision getting there?

– Perhaps the most challenging part of strategic planning is figuring out "how" to achieve the goals you identified.

For example: Create a team of experts that wins clients by delivering an exceptional experience; by doing so they becoming RAVING FANS who refer friends and family. Do so under a model that produces each team member an income and the time to live a better lifestyle than possible today.

Step 3: What desired outcome is needed to get there?

– Your outcome needs to be thought out and vetted. Ultimately your goal outcome should be:

- Essential to your success.

- Tangible and achievable.

- Measurable.

For example: By January 1, 2016, we need to be helping 39 buyers and 8 sellers a month. To make this happen for our buyers, we need to find the perfect home while expertly protecting them, negotiating the best possible price, with the least amount of stress. For our sellers, we need to utilize our proven repeatable system, based on market research, to sell their home for more than the methods of traditional agents.

<u>Step 4</u>: Creating a Priority — What action do I need to accomplish over the next 90 days to move me closer to my Goal?

– You need something that is so important that it gets special attention in your life. It is the one thing above all else that will move you closer to your goal. It should be *front and center* every single day as a commitment in your calendar.

We must create a named priority, build out the rationale and then the steps needed to achieve our goal.

For example:

Priority: Build buyer business to closed sales of 20 a month by Dec 31st 2014.

Rational: At our current conversion rate of 3%, we would need a little more than 650 leads a month, and we already produce over 700 a month.

<u>Step 5</u>: Now that we know what our Priority is, what do we need to do? In what order?

What do we attack?

- Do we generate more leads, better systems, do we hire more Buyer's Experts, or do we invest in training and develop our current Buyers Experts to increase their conversion rate…or all of the above.

- If we can do just one thing over the next 90 days, which one do we do?

- In achieving the right order to attack your priority, you have to ask yourself what success would look like. It would be success if 'xxx' happened.

For example: We would be successful if we invest in our current Buyers Experts personally and grow their knowledge, which will increase conversion and grow our monthly buyer-side deals to 20 by the end of December 2015.

Step 6: How do we measure Success?

– This is necessary in order to track your progress to your goal and measure if you were successful.

It is very important to look at Key Performance Indicators (KPI's). KPI's are quantifiable measurements, agreed to beforehand, that reflect the critical success factors of an organization.

There are leading and lagging KPI's:

- An indicator is anything that can be used to predict future financial or economic trends.

- Leading indicators – these types of indicators signal future events. Think of how a yellow light on a traffic light indicates the coming of the red light.

- Lagging Indicators – these are the ones that follow an event. The importance of a lagging indicator is its ability to confirm that a pattern is occurring or about to occur. (Unemployment is one of the most popular economic lagging indicators. If the unemployment rate is rising, it indicates that the economy has been doing poorly.)

For example: The leading KPI's for the team is unique

appointments. If an Expert Advisor has 3 unique appointments a week, this is the indicator that we will hit the lagging KPI of 1 executed contract.

Step 7: Time to keep score. How did we do?

– Assess – How did you do with your 90-day plan?

Celebrate the growth and little victories. What did we accomplish?

For example: Grew from 10 buyer-side deals a month to 15 buyer-side deals. Increased our Profit Margin 15%

What lessons did we learn?

For example: We learned that a successful Buyer's Expert advisor can write 4 or more deals a month, if allowed to specialize on just leads to appointments and appointments to open deals, and allow customer care and transaction management to bring the deal to closing.

Step 8: How do we improve?

– Now given our achievements, our strengths, opportunities, and weaknesses, how are we going to capitalize or exploit our current resources to sustain a competitive advantage? We need to focus our resources on 3 or 4 core strategies that we will employ to gain a sustainable competitive advantage.

I now have a strategic plan for my life, I know change will happen but I know that a strategic approach will see me through.

If you go to work on your goals, your goals will go to work on you.
If you go to work on your plan, your plan will go to work on you.
Whatever good things we build end up building us.
~Jim Rohn

About Shawn

Shawn W. O'Neill helps people create the life they truly want. Being bought up around a family that enjoyed working to live, not living to work, he naturally gravitated to helping others live out their perfect life. This has led him to seek out the knowledge and experience to become a strategic advisor and real estate expert, fulfilling living his life by design. He has launched Jacksonville Expert Home Advisors (JEHA) to facilitate an environment to allow others to live life to their fullest.

Shawn has been a leader in real estate over the last 12 years. He started an independent Real Estate Company and grew it to over 3 offices, and one of the top in market share – before selling out to spend more time with his family and their newly-born daughter.

Shawn was always intrigued by disruptive technology and knew the Internet would change the face of real estate. He joined a publicly-traded real estate and technology company, Zip Realty, as their regional director – leading their start-up efforts in Northeast Florida. Under his tenure, the office grew to the No. 1 office in buyer-side transactions in the region, while creating an outstanding culture of accountability and fun. He was named Director of the Year for Zip Realty. He loved "winning" while the rest of the industry was scrambling to figure out how to harness the power of the Internet to create a successful company.

Shawn O'Neill knew that his time at Zip Realty was invaluable, but he dreamed of providing real estate professionals with the time and money to live a better life, and creating an amazing experience for their clients with their proven and repeatable systems—whether it was by selling a home on time for more money, finding the best home or getting it for the best price, all with the least amount of stress.

Shawn founded the Lead Team at Exit Real Estate Gallery. This team became the No.1 team, according to the *2013 Wall Street Journal/Real Trends* reports in Florida with 394 transactions. But he knew that even though they were the No. 1 team in Florida, they were not living up to the vision he had for his top real estate team. So, he teamed up with National Association of Expert

Advisors, rebuilding his team from the ground up. He has grown from an Elite member, to a Mastermind Member and a Strategic Advisor and coach for their other members.

Shawn O'Neill graduated from Pennsylvania State University with a degree in Accounting with emphasis in Management Information Systems. His education, as well as Audit and Computer Consulting work at Deloitte and Computer Sciences Corporation, were the perfect combination to lead two start-up real estate companies.

When Shawn is not leading his teammates, or coaching his clients, he enjoys spending time with his wife Tracey, children Addison and Chase on the beach at St. Augustine, or on one of Jacksonville's 300 miles of navigable rivers.

He can be reached at :
Shawn@ExpertHomeAdvisors.com
www.facebook.com/ShawnWONeill
@ShawnWONeill on Twitter

CHAPTER 17

A DOLLAR SAVED IS *MORE* THAN A DOLLAR EARNED

BY KEVIN HU

There is no shortage of financial information. There are so many so-called financial advisors and experts out there, and everyone has their own opinions and ideas relating to money – so how do you synthesize all the information and use it to your best advantage?

My goal is not to add complexity to what seems to be an already complex financial world, but to enable everyone to understand and get ahead in the financial game. It's not that complicated, believe it or not! Once we understand the basic rules, we can use all the tools available to our advantage. The entire financial industry is trying to get your business, whether it's a bank account, line of credit or mortgage, credit card, car loan or personal loan, insurance policy or investments. It is in your best interest to be educated about a product before you buy into it.

When it comes to financial products, there are thousands of options available. A little bit of education will help you discover which products can help you save money and which will cost you in the long run. Much like choosing a vehicle, some will save you time and money, while others you know are going to cost you lots of both.

Again, it all comes back to a basic understanding of the whole financial system. How many years do we spend on our education so that we have the knowledge and skills to earn income? Easily over 10,000 hours. And how many years will we work after we graduate? Forty years, or forty-five? That's another 80,000 to 100,000 hours over our working life. Yet, shockingly, the vast majority of people spend less than 500 hours to learn about the financial tools and products that they are going to use for the rest of their life – tools that will profoundly impact their financial well-being in either a good or bad way.

I am not the strait-laced academic. However, having been in the financial industry as an insurance and investment advisor for nearly ten years, I have seen hundreds of clients. At age 32, I personally lost over $250,000 in investments and found myself needing to juggle money between seven credit cards and lines of credit, with a credit card balance close to $100,000. I've learned things in the real financial system that most advisors do not know, or will not share. I've learned what works and what tricks you can use to save yourself tens of thousands of dollars.

In our lifetime, each one of us will probably earn millions of dollars. The most important thing, however, is not how much money you make, but how much you keep in your pocket. Understand that you don't have to be a numbers wizard; what matters is understanding the concepts and how to apply them to your situation to keep the most money in your pocket.

Here are five of the most common mistakes I've encountered over the years from hundreds of clients.

1. SEPARATING YOUR MONEY AND THE BANK'S MONEY.

For most people there is a conceptual divide between the money we earn and the money we borrow from the bank. There is this notion that the money we earn is *our* money, whereas the money we owe is not. So, most people will make all their bill payments from a chequing account and put their extra money into a savings account. However, loans have evolved a lot from decades ago, and the majority of us now have what are called revolving loans, which allow us to repay the loan and re-borrow it at any time. With that perspective, why do the majority of people still put money into their savings account – which earns them practically nothing – while paying high interest on their credit cards and lines of credit?

With non-revolving loans, separating our income and our loans makes perfect sense, as we cannot withdraw the money again when we need it. The truth is, when we spend money on credit cards or lines of credit, we are actually borrowing our future earnings and using it in advance. This means, then, that if we owe the bank any money, the money we save in our savings accounts is not ours. So, why not use it to pay off the card with the highest interest rate (especially if we can always re-borrow it)? This simple step will put hundreds of after-tax dollars back into our pocket. How about using lines of credit as a chequing account instead of having a separate chequing account to pay your bills? Every dollar you temporarily park in a line of credit before paying your next bill will help you save more money on the interest.

2. KEEPING A BALANCE ACROSS A FEW CREDIT CARDS INSTEAD OF PUTTING THE WHOLE BALANCE ONTO ONE CARD.

At a financial company's grand opening, I had an opportunity to speak with one of their prospective clients. John liked the idea of using leverage to build up more assets; however, before he could consider it he would first need to get his finances in order. As we chatted, he shared that he carried a balance on two credit cards: one with a $6,000 balance on a $10,000 limit, paying 11.99% interest, and the second with a $3,200 balance on an $8,000 limit, paying 21.99% interest.

"Why don't you take the available balance from the lower interest card and pay off the higher interest one?" I asked.

"Oh no – that will make the balance over 90%, which is bad for my credit."

This is a very common mistake. We have the notion that a balance of over 90% on our credit card or line of credit is bad, and many people would rather voluntarily pay higher interest!

Actually, when you start carrying a balance on credit cards, the most important focus is not to keep the balance spread across credit cards, but to make sure not to miss any payments, and to pay the balance off as soon as possible. The difference between John's two credit cards is 10%. With the amount of $3,200, that's an extra $320 in after-tax dollars that John is paying. Wouldn't he be much better off taking that $320 interest difference and applying it to the principal instead of paying it towards interest? Not only will he pay off the balance sooner, but also he will save interest on top of interest. That $320 paid towards the principal will now save him an extra $70 on interest for the following year.

3. NOT BEING PREPARED FOR A RAINY DAY: CREDIT IS THE NAME OF THE GAME.

We have all heard the recommendation to save up 3-6 months of income for emergencies. Since it doesn't make sense to amass money in a savings account while still having a balance on the loans, the use of credit becomes extremely important.

Credit – interestingly, when you don't need it, banks will gladly issue you more; however, when you desperately need it, banks will be reluctant to approve it.

This is why it's important to know that credit, like insurance, needs to be established well beforehand. I've been building up my credit since I was eighteen, paying my balance off every month and never missing a payment. Often, the bank has offered to raise my credit limit, and I would always accept. As I mentioned previously, due to my investment loss, I now have close to a $100,000 balance on my credit cards. However, I don't pay 20% interest on my credit cards; my average interest rate is less than 7%. I have a $28,000 balance on one credit card, and over the last four years I've paid less than 2% interest on it – the first two years at 0% and the past two years at 1.99%. I also have a few other cards with interest rates ranging from 1.0% to 2.99%. Imagine how much money I've saved on interest by understanding a few simple tricks. Credit is not meant for you to spend money in advance and then pay 20% interest on it, but to help carry you through tough times.

4. FOCUSING ON A LUMP SUM OF MONEY INSTEAD OF A MONTHLY RECURRING INCOME.

If you could choose between a $1 million lump sum and a $6,000 per month guaranteed income for life, which would you choose? Believe it or not, many people would opt for the million-dollar lump sum instead of the monthly income. Having been in the financial industry for nearly ten years, I find it ironic that, on one hand, advisors tell clients that they need to prepare for their retirement or for financial freedom, and on the other hand they tell them that they should accumulate a million dollars in order not to outlive their money. The rationale is that once you accumulate a million dollars and put it into a conservative investment that gives a 5% rate of return, you will have $50,000 a year as income without touching your principal.

We need to understand that there is a big difference between getting a 5% rate of return and finding an investment that will produce a 5% income year after year. After all, there is no guarantee with any type of investment, even so-called conservative ones. Those who experienced the tech bubble burst in 2000 or the financial meltdown in 2008 will undoubtedly agree. Let me explain further.

Using the example of a million dollars: the goal is to have $50,000 annual income to live on, which can be achieved with a 5% rate of return. However, during the 2008 crash, even the conservative funds lost between 20%-30%. Using the median loss of 25%, this million dollars is left as $750,000. Now, not only does it need a 34% rate of return to recover the loss, but a 5% return will now only generate $37,500 – a shortfall of $12,500 per year. If we take the shortfall from the principal, it's going to reduce the principal, which in turn will reduce the income that will be generated in future years.

Instead, with the same million dollars, find an investment that will generate $50,000 a year in income – like dividends from shares, or rental income. A drop in the market value on such an investment does not affect the income it's generating, as it's not based on the value but on the number of shares you own, or on the rental unit. So, even if the value never recovers, as long as you continue to receive that

$50,000 income, you will never outlive your money. Don't focus on accumulating a lump sum of money; focus on generating recurring income. Financial freedom is when you are able to replace your employment income with income from investments or a business, so that you can have more time to spend with family and do the things you desire to do.

5. PAYING THE CANADIAN REVENUE AGENCY MORE THAN YOU NEED TO.

As the saying goes: "there are two things guaranteed in life: death and taxes."

We may not have control over death, but tax is something everyone should take control of. It is the single greatest expense in our life – not our education, home, vehicles, or children. In North America, employees pay an average of 25-30% of their income to the government as income tax. Imagine: every year, the first three to four months of your salary goes to the government as tax. If you are making $16 an hour, you only get to use $11.20 to $12.00 out of that $16 dollars.

That said, not everything is created equal, especially when it comes to the tax system. There are two types of tax systems that have been created, one for employees and another for business owners. The major difference between the two is that employees earn money, pay tax, then spend what is left over, while business owners earn money, spend it, then pay tax on what is left over. For example, a business owner makes $60,000 a year and used $40,000 as expenses, then pays tax on the leftover amount, in this case $20,000. At 25% tax that's $5,000 paid as income tax. In contrast, an employee who makes the same $60,000 a year pays $15,000 (25%) as income tax and is left with $45,000 to use.

As a business owner, you are allowed by the government to convert part of your common expenses – gas, car insurance, cell phone, office supplies, gifts, dining out, entertainment, Internet, travel, and many others – into your business expenses, as some of these can be used to help grow your business and increase profits.

Starting a business doesn't have to cost a lot of money! It is possible to start a home-based business with a few hundred dollars and less than $50 a month to maintain. I'm referring here to network marketing, which admittedly requires liberal amounts of caution, critical thinking, and common sense. There are more multi-level marketing companies cropping up than any one person can keep track of, and I'm aware of many unsavories. However, this simple step could save you tens of thousands of dollars for years to come.

When starting a home-based business, beware of overspending by buying the biggest package. The network marketing industry sells dreams, but like every other business, only 5% of people ever become truly successful in the industry. Start small and work your way up. A home-based business is considered a business, so now you can enjoy the tax benefits that every business owner is enjoying.

Always keep in mind that any after-tax dollar you save is equivalent to $1.30-1.40 you need to earn pretax. If you can save $5,000 in interest, fees, and taxes, that's equivalent to working twelve weeks fulltime at $15 an hour, which is $7,200 pretax dollars. That is why *a dollar saved is more than a dollar earned.*

About Kevin

Kevin Hu started working at age 16. He has worked at restaurants, a travel agency, a supermarket, and a mattress factory. He quickly realized that his passion was to go into business, to have businesses that would generate a steady income to support his family and, at the same time, support orphanages and charities.

One of Kevin's biggest desires is to support orphans and children. He strongly believes in the Biblical proverb: "train up a child in the way he should go, and when he is old he will not depart from it."

Kevin started working in the financial industry at age 24. He has a head for numbers and he enjoyed showing clients strategies to not only increase cashflow and reduce expenses, but also to decrease taxes by starting a business. With this unique approach, in 2007, 2008, and 2009, Kevin qualified as a member of the Million Dollar Round Table, among the top 5% in the insurance industry.

During the 2008 financial meltdown, Kevin, at age 28, was able to pull out both his and his clients' investments from the equity market before the market crash to avoid any losses, avoiding one of the biggest financial meltdowns in history. Kevin thought he was on top of the world, until in one investment in 2010, he lost over $150,000; desperate to recuperate the losses, he lost another $100,000 in 2012. For over a year, Kevin struggled with depression, and in 2013 he decided to resign from the insurance and investment industry. Still devastated from the losses, Kevin wasn't sure what he wanted to do. He moved into many home-based business ventures, mainly because of the dream the industry promised.

In June 2014, Kevin attended one of Colin Sprake's workshops, "Business Excellence." During the workshop, he was able to meet some of the world's best speakers, trainers, and business experts: Robert Allan, Croix Sather, Nick Psaila, Thomas Bähler, Viveka von Rosen, Nick Nanton, and Joel Comm. From them, Kevin realized that through his unique skills and experiences he could bring value to individuals and families. He could coach them through financial struggles, especially considering how the majority of families are living paycheque-to-paycheque and are 3-6 months away from bankruptcy if they became unemployed.

In June 2014, Kevin founded Top Money Coach Inc. to educate individuals and families to better understand the Canadian financial system. Kevin coaches them on the myriad of products and tools available, helping them easily put thousands of dollars back into their pockets.

You can connect with Kevin at:
Tel: 604-992-8778
kevin@topmoneycoach.ca
www.topmoneycoach.ca
www.facebook.com/topmoneycoach.ca

CHAPTER 18

SAY YES!

BY SALLY DIETTERLE

I recently had the privilege of listening to a speech that Jim Carrey gave at the 2014 MUM graduation. He talked about how his dad could have been a great comedian, but because he was afraid of failing, he chose instead a "safe and secure" job as an accountant. After 12 years of giving himself loyally to that firm he was let go, and their family went through a terrible period of time just trying to survive.

Jim describes what he learned from that experience and it was this: that you can fail at what you *don't* want, so you might as well take the chance at doing what you love. Isn't that great? How true that you can fail just as easily doing something that you don't love, as you can fail at doing something that you do love. Life does not offer us any guarantees. We might never live long enough to collect that pension that we are so diligently paying into every month. Or, heaven forbid, we could end up with an injury that would render us unable to continue working, so we might as well spend what time we have doing something that brings us joy.

Some of us know early on how we want to spend our days in our adult life. Others of us need to have more life experiences before we can figure that out. I fall into the latter group. I need to try *lots* of things before I find something that resonates with my soul. It's because of this that I developed a "say YES" attitude. I make a habit to say YES to just about every opportunity that comes along. I've learned that what shows up in our lives as a result of saying YES is often far greater that we could have ever dreamed up ourselves.

I think the first big thing I can remember saying YES to was getting married at 16 years old. Subsequently, I then said YES to have four children in 5.5 years. By the time I was 23 years old, I had a newborn, a two-year-old with a broken leg, a four-year-old and a five-and-a-half-year-old about to start kindergarten. As you can imagine, I didn't have a lot of extra time to sit, let alone sit and dream. But on the rare occasion that I did allow myself to dream, I dreamed of one thing. And that dream was to own a business. I knew for certain that one day I'd do that. I didn't have a clue what type of business I wanted and because I'm a YES girl, I didn't want to restrict my options, so I left them wide open with just leaving it at "own a business" – whatever that looked like.

When you're not specific with the Universe about what you want, it tends to have quite a sense of humor as it attempts to get you to define what it is that you really want. So over the next decade, what owning a business came to look like was me trying my hand at almost every home-based business available at the time. I sold everything from Mary K to a children's clothing line, crafting kits, Princess House crystal and finally, Tupperware. I became adept at reading The Big Hungry Bear to nicely-dressed children who sat on homemade embroidered cushions and ate their snacks from little crystal plates, while sipping out of Tupperware cups with lids. I didn't stick with any of these ideas long enough to become successful, because deep down they didn't resonate with my soul's true desire.

So a decade later when I found myself facing parenting alone without any means of support, I had to stop playing at this home-based business thing and actually find a way to make money so I could support my family. My dream of owning a business was still there, but I hadn't found the perfect fit for me and I wanted the security of having a regular paycheck. I landed a job as a 911 operator for the local police department and I worked long and hard 48-60 hours a week just to feed my family. I bought and sold my house more times than I care to remember, each time refinancing so that I could pull out a little bit of equity in order to provide just a little bit more for my family.

Similar to Jim Carrey's dad, my safe job came to an end after seven years, but not because I was laid off, but because the long hours and stress of the job took its toll on me as I silently battled PTSD. It was then I knew what it meant to fail at something that you don't want.

Sometimes, we need to quit things in order to make room for new things to come along. There's a big difference between quitting and giving up. If something isn't working in your life then you owe it to yourself, your loved ones and to the universe to change it. Our country is filled with people who are riddled with disease and poor health, because they are doing things that they don't love doing. You can ignore the early signs of depression and being over-stressed only so long, and then the body begins to systematically shut down one system at a time – until we are forced to make a major change or risk an early death.

One day, after I had quit my job, I was having a wonderful full body massage at one of those Spas that delights all your senses. The kind that smells heavenly, where the soft music washes over you and you can experience five minutes of peace and quiet without one of the children barging in and making their emergency your emergency. Being there relaxed me and allowed me time to dream again. It didn't come as a surprise to anyone when I announced shortly after that I was going back to school to become an esthetician so that I could open my own Spa. Eleven months later, I opened Blackberries and I thought it was my dream come true. It soon become apparent, however, that I was much more moved when I was the one *getting* the massage instead of the one *giving* the massage. It was time to come up with a plan B. I forced myself to define what it was that I wanted, as well as what I didn't want, from owning a business. That experience gave me the opportunity to get really clear about what it was that created a spark in me.

You see, the universe *wants* to deliver, but it needs us to be clear about what dream we want it to deliver. If we're not clear, it just keeps pulling things out of a hat in an attempt to see if it's getting close to what we're looking for.

I believe that it was not a coincidence that after I got clear about what I wanted, the universe delivered in a big way. Everyone in my life knew that I was looking for a business opportunity. I talked about it all the time. So I wasn't a surprise to me when one Thursday evening at about 5 p.m. when I was home alone, I got a call from my step dad saying that my brother, who owned a transport company, had just verbally agreed to sell out to the competition for very little money. No one would keep their jobs; they just wanted the customer list, phone number and name. Now, this was a company that although quite poorly run, had something special about it as there were many employees as well as customers that had been with the company since its inception 23 years prior.

Although I had worked as a driver for them for about two years, I knew absolutely NOTHING about running a transport Company. But my "say YES" spirit rose up and I thought, hey, if he can sell to them then he can sell to me. Only I was willing to make it even easier for him by absorbing the entire obligation of the company such as the leaseholds and the monthly contracts. All he had to do was sign it over to me and I'd agree to keep everyone employed and keep the customers from experiencing any disruption to their service level. In addition, I agreed to give him a certain dollar amount each month until I had paid him his asking price in full. That way I didn't need to come up with a bunch of cash that I didn't have and he had assurance that he had income coming in every month. By 11 a.m. the next morning we had a deal drawn up for immediate acquisition, and I was not only a business owner but I was also on my way that afternoon to Mexico with a friend who had invited me prior to join them for a week aboard their "boat" that turned out to be a 100 foot yacht in La Paz. "Say YES!"

I felt very sure of my decision until I told my best friend that I bought the company and she thought I'd lost my mind. It's interesting to me that even though the people that I'm close to in my life all knew that I had this dream, once I signed the papers they all thought I was crazy. Maybe they thought I was crazy/brave, or maybe crazy/inspiring but definitely crazy. Throughout our life, there will always be people who think we're crazy but it's important to remember that it's our own journey. No one can walk it for us. And we can't let other people's opinions of what we're doing define our experience or hold us back from living our dreams.

It's been five-and-a-half years now since my journey began as a female entrepreneur in a man's industry, but I haven't let the *status quo* define or alter the vision that I have for the company. I have a big vision for the company, but mostly I just want to know that I'm making a difference in people's lives every day. Whether that is as simple as getting someone's merchandise delivered on time, or making sure that each driver is making a decent living, or taking a few extra moments to listen and connect with a customer or staff member that is going through a hard time. The little things add up to big things. On a hot summer day, I'm sometimes out in my jeep with the top down (that's different than with my top OFF!) and I have a cooler in the back filled with cold water or lemonade that I take around to some of my customers. Other times I'm in the office answering the phones, taking the daily orders where I get to talk to customers who remember that as much as 5 years ago I came around to their place of business with cold water. People remember the little things; *people buy from people they know and like.*

It took me quite a while to figure out that out. But that's how many successful entrepreneurs make a difference in their business, their communities and in the lives of their customers. People want to *know* you and *like* you before they'll do business with you. Perhaps I would have been more successful selling Tupperware if I'd have learned that lesson sooner. But I believe that this journey is a constant lesson in doing our best and then releasing all attachment to the outcome. Will I be successful 10 years from now? I don't know; there are no guarantees, but each day gives me another chance to get things as right as I can…a chance to make a difference…a chance to do something that I really love. And if I fail at that then at least I failed doing something that I love instead of at something that I didn't. And that's all we can really hope for. So what will *you* do with your *one* wild and precious life?

About Sally

Sally Dietterle is the owner of StreetHawk Express, a local cartage company that delivers commercial goods around the lower mainland of BC. She is responsible for the livelihood of around 25 people in her employ. Although she prefers to be trekking across a foreign country or hanging out on her boyfriend's boat in Florida, she has her roots set down in beautiful Langley, BC Canada. She is currently living alone for the first time in her life and arrives home every day with gratitude that her house stayed clean all day while she was away. When she's not out delivering cold lemonade or fresh baked cookies to her customers, she keeps busy by bossing people around at the office, especially her two middle children who both work full-time with her at StreetHawk.

Sally is a grandmother to two of the cutest little boys in the world, and although people often mistake her for the boys' mother, she flashes her grandmother badge with honour whenever possible. She considers herself blessed to live near all four of her children and can often be found spending leisure time with them. She practices hot yoga almost daily in the hope that she will be able to stay active for many years, and one day is able to hike some of the world's greatest hikes with her grandsons.

Writing has been a passion of hers for many years, but was never really practiced beyond cards and notes to her friends or the annual Christmas letter about the shenanigans of her crazy household. When she announced that she intended to walk over 800 km in 31 days on the Camino de Santiago, Spain in 2013, her friends and family encouraged her to keep a blog of her journey. She reluctantly did just that and her blog of that journey as well as other musings can be read at www.livealifeyouwillenjoylookingbackon.com. Sally enjoys most of her recent adventures alongside her boyfriend John whom she met while walking the Camino. They both love international travel and hiking or just hanging out on the boat in Florida or the Bahamas. Although they live diagonally across the continent from each other, having monthly adventures to look forward to adds a lot of excitement to their lives and gives her some great material to blog about. Both of them being entrepreneurs gives them the freedom to get away regularly and they wouldn't trade it for the world.

Sally's last big adventure was in September 2014 where she travelled first to Germany with her 81 year old father and two sisters. After visiting western Germany and meeting members of her dad's family, they made their way to France where they met up with John and her sisters husband, Bill, and then toured the D-Day beaches in Normandy and laid flowers on the grave of four soldiers who lost their lives and dreams in the hope that the rest of us could keep ours. Bless their souls…. may we never forget their sacrifice.

CHAPTER 19

SLEEPING TO SUCCESS

PATRICIA E. TAKACS, D.M.D.

What is success? According to the World English Dictionary, success is defined as the favorable outcome of something attempted, or as the attainment of wealth, fame, etc. How we define success will depend on what our goals are: money, education, sports, politics? It also will depend on how old we are when we achieve success. One thing is certain, sleep is an integral part of the road to success.

I'm sure you would agree that the following people are considered to be successful in their respective fields: Rosie O'Donnell, Shaquille O'Neill, Regis Philbin, Rick Perry, and William Shatner. What they all have in common is that they have sleep apnea. NFL great Reggie White and Jerry Garcia of the Grateful Dead both died in their sleep from sleep apnea. Sleep apnea is defined as a sleep disordered breathing in which the sleeper stops breathing longer than 10 seconds at any given time. The more times this occurs while sleeping, the greater the risk of detrimental damage to our body. If left untreated, it will lead to an increase risk of stroke, high blood pressure, heart attack, Type II Diabetes, GERD, fibromyalgia, atrial fibrillation, dementia, and ultimately premature death.

Sleep Disordered Breathing (SDB) includes snoring. And Obstructive Sleep Apnea (OSA) is not only a phenomenon of adults, but of children as well. What does this all have to do with success? Good quality sleep is essential for healthy bodies. "Deep sleep" or Delta sleep, is the most important stage and makes up from 10-25% of our total sleep. As we age, this number decreases. However, in children, it accounts for 40-50% of sleep and is it is during this time that the peak levels of Growth Hormone are reached and when most body and cell recovery occurs. Therefore, a child who has sleep disordered breathing, which includes snoring, will tend to exhibit childhood obesity, learning and behavioral issues, failure to thrive and some hormonal and metabolic problems. Any and all of these consequences of poor quality sleep in children will negatively affect their future successes as they reach adulthood and beyond.

Many symptoms of sleep disordered breathing in children are very similar to those of ADHD and can be indistinguishable and therefore misdiagnosed. Is the problem of paying attention and concentrating and lack of organization due to ADHD or is it really the result of poor sleep, and thus a "sleepy" child? Children with obstructive sleep apnea have increased rate of behavioral problems at home and at school, thus affecting learning and resulting in low academic performance. They may also be aggressive and unwilling to follow established rules. The question then becomes: are we dealing with poor sleep yet treating for ADHD? And as the child reaches adulthood and is still being "treated" for ADHD, they may have symptoms of sleep disordered breathing that result in difficulty concentrating and completing tasks, poor organizational skills and memory lapses. All would affect the ability of the person to achieve business and personal success.

So what is the role of the dentist in assessing the consequences of obstructive sleep apnea in kids and its possible link to ADHD? Sleep apnea occurs when the tongue drops back and obstructs the airway while sleeping. By looking at the shape of children's jaws, dentists are able to intervene and begin early expansion of the upper jaw so to allow the lower jaw the ability to grow and fit. This in turn makes a mouth that was too small for the tongue, now able to accommodate the tongue and thus keep it from dropping back into the throat. If a child has a recessed upper and lower jaw, then both jaws should be advanced as soon as it is diagnosed and treated as young as age 1. Proper referrals to pediatric dentists and orthodontists are imperative. Correction of back teeth crossbite should also be done as soon as it is discovered during a routine dental exam. This allows for expansion of the upper jaw and more room for growth and development. Children should be examined and treated to correct developmental problems at a young age, 7-9, and not wait until all of the permanent teeth have come in and most jaw growth is complete.

If a child is a mouth breather, their facial growth is affected by a narrow upper arch, long face and increased likelihood of sleep problems. There is no physiologic benefit through breathing through the mouth. Air is filtered and warmed when breathing through the nose, and is important for the release of nitric acid which prevents bacterial growth and helps the lungs absorb oxygen.

Examining the tonsils and adenoids and making timely referrals to an ENT for early removal will also allow for a more open airway while sleeping. This surgery has been shown to eliminate sleep apnea in 70-90% of children. Checking for signs of grinding on the baby teeth and first permanent molars, along with behavioral problems, large tonsils and adenoids, and snoring all indicate the potential for sleep disordered breathing and possible sleep apnea. If a child is a chronic bedwetter, often has bad dreams and snores, the probability that there is obstructive sleep apnea increases. We must ask if the child has chronic ear infections and/or tubes as this also is suggestive of a poorly developed upper jaw and Eustachian tube.

Parents need to understand that the signs of sleep disordered breathing and ADHD are indistinguishable from each other. A thorough and early dental exam of children as young as age 1 is imperative to look for jaw development issues and treated or referred to the appropriate medical or dental specialist. Prevention of a misdiagnosis of ADHD and its concomitant social stigma as well as the prescribing of Ritalin, when instead, it is a poor sleep issue, is important. Sleep deprivation results in a sense of exhaustion during the day. By taking Ritalin, sleep is affected negatively, thus promoting the vicious cycle of poor sleep hygiene.

Quality sleep is truly the road to success. We must begin to treat the problem and not the symptoms. Untreated sleep apnea can lead to a host of developmental, social and behavioral problems throughout life. An increased risk of developing a host of other health problems rises exponentially. And ultimately, left untreated, sleep apnea will result in premature death.

As a general dentist, I am at the forefront of being able to help my patients live longer, healthier lives and improve their quality of life. We accomplish this by teaching the importance of healthy gums and teeth to prevent heart disease, stroke and increased blood pressure. We provide beauty when desired and the ability to function, eat and speak. We are forever challenged by the myriad of medicines our patients take in order to control their medical problems.

Part of my responsibility to my patients is to assess whether they may have an underlying sleep problem. This is done through questionnaires about how they sleep and how they feel during the day, whether they snore or gasp while they sleep, types of headaches, jaw pain and noises. An in-depth dental and medical history exam are done and the amount of medication taken to control chronic diseases are evaluated. Combine this information with a thorough exam of the tongue, checking for scalloping and size, the size and shape of the tonsils, the condition of the uvula, if it is elongated, and wear of the teeth and recession of the gums, and we can be pretty confident to pronounce if there might be an underlying sleep apnea problem.

Reggie White played 15 seasons of professional football for the Philadelphia Eagles and the Green Bay Packers and retired in 2000. He was a Pro Bowl and All-Pro defensive player and also became an ordained minister during his playing career. He was selected to the Pro Football Hall of Fame as well as the College Football Hall of Fame where he played at Tennessee.

The day after Christmas, 2004, at the age of 43, he was rushed to the hospital from his home and pronounced dead. The cause of death was a fatal cardiac arrhythmia, partly as a result of untreated sleep apnea.

Jerry Garcia of the Grateful Dead, died in his sleep at age 53, of a heart attack contributed by drug addiction and sleep apnea and diabetes.

CONNOR

Connor was labeled a "troubled kid" by age 10. He had always been a difficult child growing up and was demanding and temperamental. He would often throw full-blown temper tantrums at home and at school and had such low self-esteem that he would often proclaim that "I wish I was dead." His grades were so low that the school threatened to kick him out of 4th grade. He was always being a bully to someone and there never was a trigger that prompted his outbursts. One day he might be perfectly normal and do as was asked, the next day he would roll on the floor in a full tantrum and would need several hours to calm down. Because he refused to conform to rules, he was put in a special program and then the search began to find out what was wrong with him. After a series of tests, he was found to have several allergies to trees and pets; he had sleep disordered breathing and night grinding, and was evaluated by a dentist that indicated he had a narrow palate and enlarged tonsils and adenoids.

Due to his allergies and the poor development of his jaws, Connor was a mouth breather. This long term breathing pattern changed the shape of his face and jaws and affected the development of his airway. After removal of his tonsils and adenoids and development of his jaws, and being put on allergy medication, he finally was able to sleep through the night. Suddenly, his behavior improved as did his grades. The fact was that Connor was sleep-deprived, not attention deficit. By opening his airway and allowing him to breathe through his nose at night, he began to flourish. Connor's only problem was that he struggled to breathe while he was sleeping. Yet, he had been labeled from a very young age as a "troubled kid." Instead of a report card of D's and F's, Connor now brings home consistent A's and B's. He is well on his way to success!

As a dentist on the forefront of treating not just tooth decay and gum disease, I have embraced the concept that good oral health is critical to good health and long life. The mouth is the gateway to the overall health of our bodies. Most of you have read about the connection of periodontal disease to heart disease and stroke. But you probably were not aware of the effects of acid reflux on your teeth or that this could be one symptom of obstructed sleep apnea. The acid eats away the chewing surfaces of your teeth and the backs of the upper front teeth. Combine this with chipped edges on your front teeth and we find another sign of possible sleep apnea. Attempting to open your airway while you sleep by moving your lower jaw forward to move the tongue out of the way results in this breakdown. You notice that the wear on your teeth is getting worse, that you are waking up with headaches and that by mid morning you are moody and tired, you may have sleep apnea. Often, people who complain of chronic headaches, facial pain and TMJ pain have an underlying sleep problem. The pain exacerbates at night and prevents you from getting a good, restorative sleep.

A good night's sleep is a luxury. Sleep disordered breathing will cause a myriad of problems for people during the day, including falling asleep at work, forgetfulness and lack of organization. How's that look for a successful business career? Combine that with the host of medical problems that will arise and you are now looking at a potentially life threatening condition that can be easily treated, if your healthcare provider or your dentist will make the connection.

Snoring isn't normal and may very well be the first outward sign of a potentially life threatening condition called Obstructive Sleep Apnea. My goal of this chapter is to make you aware of how important sleep is for quality of life. Success begins with sleep. If you suspect you may have sleep apnea or that your child may have sleep apnea, I encourage you to visit your physician and your dentist and ask questions and seek answers. Sleep apnea is treated by a sleep physician, with C-PAP, a mask that is worn at night, or by a qualified dentist with an oral appliance. This is a medical device and should be covered by medical insurance. Surgery is a last resort but may be the only option for uncontrolled sleep problems.

For further information, I encourage you to go online and search "sleep apnea and ADHD" as well as "health consequences of sleep apnea."

About Patricia

Dr. Trish Takacs is a 1983 graduate from the University of Kentucky College of Dentistry and maintains a private practice in cosmetic and general dentistry – Beaumont Family Dentistry, in Lexington, KY. Her interests lie in reconstruction for patients with worn down dentition, chronic head and neck pain, and sleep apnea. The primary focus of Beaumont Family Dentistry is to provide comprehensive care for each patient, not limited to oral care needs, but including the overall physical health of each patient.

She and her husband have been married for 33 years and have a son and daughter. Her son is a 2012 graduate of UK College of Dentistry and is an associate at Beaumont Family Dentistry and her daughter will be graduating from the Dental College in 2015. Her outside interests include golf and reading, and hanging out with the family dogs.

CHAPTER 20

GOING BEYOND PASSION: THE KEYS TO ENTREPRENEURIAL SUCCESS

BY JACK HANSON

When you're 35, broke, with no prospects in sight, it's easy to lose your passion for…well, passion.

What do I mean by that? Simply this – today, it seems like almost everyone is advising you to follow your passion and build a business around it. Do an Internet search on "turning your passion into a successful business" and you will get, no kidding, over 62 million hits. Try it yourself if you don't believe me.

So-called success coaches love to tell you to "do what you love," because that will bring you the riches you've been waiting for. And popular culture is a big contributor to this philosophy – how many movies and TV shows portray protagonists who leave the cold, faceless corporate world for where their heart leads them and become huge success stories as a result?

Well, I'm here to tell you some good news and some bad news on the subject. Let's get the bad news out of the way first: Passion is not the answer to everything. If you absolutely love, love, LOVE to, say, paint miniature birdhouses, you're going to find it hard to support yourself (let alone a family) on that! Back in the day, something like that used to be called a "hobby" – which was what you did *after* work – not *for* work!

So what's the good news?

The good news is you can instead tap into who you truly are, what your skillset is and valuable relationships you build - and create a true, lasting and *satisfying* personal success.

I'm the living proof of that.

When I left that "faceless" corporate world at the age of 35, it wasn't to follow my dreams. It actually wasn't my choice – I was laid off, and frankly, I didn't know how I was going to make a living! What I *did* know, however, was that I no longer wanted to be at the mercy of that corporate world any longer that had pulled the rug out from under me too many times before.

That's why my *real* passion was to control my own destiny and be my own boss.

Now, I knew instinctively I couldn't do that by "following my heart." It wasn't realistic or attainable; like anybody else, I had to make enough money to live on. What I *could* do however, was leverage my talents, experience and relationships to build a new business.

That led me to Home Owner Association (HOA) Management.

Was I passionate about HOAs? I'm not sure anybody is. BUT...I was good at managing them. It fit my skillset. And I had ten years of experience networking with the kind of land development professionals that were perfectly positioned to help me launch my own business. That business became Melrose Management Partnership, and, ultimately, it made me a millionaire.

So, no, I didn't follow my passion – instead, I followed what I knew I could do and succeed at. And now, after 18 years of hard work as a business owner, I'm recognized as a leading authority in my field and am able to enjoy an amazing lifestyle. Not only that, but I'm getting ready to franchise my company to others who want to experience the same amazing level of success I have through HOA management.

And when you do that - you can afford to paint all the miniature birdhouses you'd like!

KEYS TO BUILDING YOUR OWN SUCCESSFUL BUSINESS

Okay, I kid about painting birdhouses, but the truth is that many can (and do) follow their dreams and make a business out of it too. My dream just happened to be to own my own business and make it as successful as possible as quickly as possible.

The question becomes, do you just want to focus only on what you *want* to do for a profession – or do you want to focus on controlling your own destiny and becoming a successful entrepreneur? Rarely do both things come together and it's an incredible gift when they do. But the thing is, if you run your own successful business, chances are you will have more time and more resources to enjoy your other true passions. If you don't? You will be at the mercy of others and perhaps struggle for a good income.

I'd like to help you avoid that. In the remainder of this chapter, I'd like to share some "Power Principles" I discovered to be true for me and that will be useful to those of you who also want to become prosperous entrepreneurs.

BE REALISTIC ABOUT YOUR PASSIONS AND DREAMS

You may be passionate about, say, music, art, books, or movies. But, unless you are an instant prodigy whose special qualities are immediately recognized, you have to face the fact that it will take you a long time to succeed in these fields – if you're able to do it at all.

Traditionally, the age to go after these kinds of "impossible dreams" is when you're young, so you still have enough time to change career direction. And that's fine. But at some point, you should face the reality that, if you want to have a comfortable life, you need to make money. That means you may have to work at something you don't necessarily *love,* but you are skilled at doing. And, again, a successful business can easily accommodate a part-time passion.

How do you determine whether your passion can sustain a business that will support you financially? That's our next Power Principle.

EVALUATE YOUR CURRENT POSITION

In addition to analyzing your most heartfelt ambitions, also realistically appraise your current situation, so you can gain the most insight into what business opportunities you can best take advantage of.

Here's a short checklist you should work through:

✓ **Who do you know?** To me, relationships can be the most important aspect of building a business. Identify your specific network of people, what business they're in and what value they might be able to bring to whatever your new venture might be.

✓ **What do you know?** Think about everything from what you learned in school to the knowledge you've gained from job and life experience. Whatever your business turns out to be, it's best if it matches up with your skillset/knowledge base.

✓ **What are your financial resources and limitations?** If you're a 22-year-old with no real responsibilities, you obviously have a lot more time and leeway to chase a dream. Who cares if you're waiting on tables while going on acting auditions? If, however, you're in your 30's with a spouse and kids, that's a whole different story – and one that could have an unhappy ending if you're not honest about your situation.

Match the answers to these questions against your passion. Do you have the necessary contacts to make some headway? Have you developed your talents and knowledge sufficiently? And can you afford to go for your dreams? If the answers come down too heavily on the negative side, you might want to consider pursuing a more realistic business.

LEVERAGE YOUR RELATIONSHIPS

Whatever direction your business takes, your network of business associates and even family and friends will most likely be your most important assets. The right people can open the right doors for you - so treat those relationships like fine china: *Always be aware of how valuable they are as well as how easily they can break.*

The best way to honor relationships is to practice the law of reciprocity – the more you do for other people, the more they will do for you. The most powerful business alliances are created when both parties' self-interests overlap – so always think about how you can best serve those in a position to help you along.

Also, remember to always tend to relationships so they can blossom and grow. If you don't, there's a good chance they will stagnate or even wither and die. Successful relationships take work and dedication, just like anything else.

At the same time, honestly evaluate every relationship on a regular basis to make sure that relationship is still important to your progress. There will be times when someone might drop you because they don't see any benefit to them; you too should do the same, unless you have an actual personal friendship with the person you'd like to continue. It's okay to disconnect when you feel the need.

Finally, remember that one relationship should lead to another. If you properly build a strong professional network, you'll find yourself exponentially expanding your reach.

UNDERSTAND THAT AUTHENTICITY
IS ESSENTIAL TO SUCCESS

Lest you think the previous section was all about how to ruthlessly "work" people to your own advantage and pretend to be something you're not, let me assure you – that is NOT the case.

In fact, the only way to develop and build strong relationships is to be **an authentic person at all times.** Anything less will result in a bad reputation – and perhaps a bad business outcome. For my part, I can safely say that I've developed an ability in business settings to smell a phony a mile away. Most successful entrepreneurs develop that "sixth sense" – they have to or they get burnt way too often.

Here are some critical "Keys to Authenticity":

- **Know what you're talking about.** If you're not 100% sure of an answer when someone asks you a question, let them know you'll find out for sure and get back to them. When you spread false or compromised information, it diminishes your credibility and the perception of your expertise.

- **Be humble and listen.** You can learn a great deal more by listening rather than talking – as a matter of fact, you'll be amazed how much you'll find out. Take the time to fully hear out someone and make sure you completely understand what they're saying. And remember, the more you let another person talk, the more that person will inadvertently reveal about themselves.

- **Be respectful**. People like it when you genuinely make them feel important and special. It may only take a handshake and a question about how their family is doing, but little things add up.

- **Be truthful with others**. It only takes one lie to damage the trust in a relationship – and, depending on how damaging the lie is, to possibly destroy the relationship all together. It's not worth taking the risk. A pattern of dishonesty will ultimately lead to you not being taken seriously.

- **Be truthful with yourself**. It can be just as damaging to a business venture to lie to yourself as it is to lie to others. When you convince yourself you're doing better than you are, you don't take necessary steps to correct a downturn. When you convince yourself you're doing worse than you are, you don't take proper advantage of success. Try to achieve an objective balance in your self-perception and ask others you trust for feedback to ensure you have it.

AVOID FEELING ENTITLED AT ALL COSTS

Dr. Steve Maraboli once said, "Beware: it is a quick transition from a nourishing sense of gratitude to a poisonous sense of entitlement." And I agree – the biggest lesson I ever learned was anyone who truly believes everyone owes them something is a fool. This feeling can quickly overtake you as you become more successful, and it's especially dangerous because it's hard to see coming at you.

How can you combat it? Easy. Do what I discussed in the last section and *be honest with yourself.* If you can't do that without help, again, turn to a close friend or confidant that will make a commitment to telling you what you need to hear.

CONNECT THE DOTS

You probably already know the story about the elephant and the group of blind men tasked to describe the animal. Each one felt a different section of the animal, so, in turn each one described a totally different animal. The only way to understand the elephant's shape was to get input from *each one* of the group.

In business, you can easily have the same kind of tunnel vision. You might focus on the competition without looking at consumer demand. You might be obsessed with your costs going up without noticing that what's happening in the marketplace. When you are only rigorously analyzing one area of your business, you are capable of making disastrous decisions. That's why you must connect *all* the dots before you make any kind of major changes or adjustments.

At the same time, you also have to understand that everyone makes mistakes, including you. Encourage everyone around you to admit their mistakes and don't be shy about admitting yours. It adds to your authenticity, especially if you take the steps to fix the problem and ensure the same mistake isn't made again. This is something I pride myself on doing and hope you will as well.

ALWAYS HEDGE YOUR BETS

"Hedging" is a tactical risk management strategy used in limiting or offsetting probability of loss. It's a transfer of risk similar to buying an insurance policy and it's a very important concept that has served me well.

Whenever I embarked on a new venture, I always made sure I had some sort of side income before moving forward. I didn't want to run out of any resources if the newest business prospect failed for some reason.

Psychologically, it's also important to be properly bankrolled. Starting a business is incredibly stressful and you have to be at the top of your game. When you try to do it with little or no money, your self-worth is low and anxiety level high. That makes it hard to concentrate on making your new enterprise succeed. Don't jump into a new business with all confidence and no capital.

STAY IN CONTROL OF YOUR OWN
DESTINY AT ALL TIMES

This is the principle that more than ever has become the most important objective in my life. If there was only one piece of wisdom that I would want you to take from this chapter, it would be that being a business owner allows you to control your own destiny; for better or for worse. If you'll excuse my bluntness, I've found that I would rather work for ten inconsiderate idiots than one. When you have an inconsiderate idiot for a boss and maybe he doesn't like the shoes you wear to work one day, he can fire you on the spot. However, when it's your company, and you have ten inconsiderate idiots for clients, you can lose one and still be okay.

I certainly don't mean to infer that everyone is an inconsiderate idiot – but you've probably already run into your fair share of them. If you maintain a large enough network and client base, however, you'll also enjoy working with a lot of awesome, great people, as I have.

I'm excited to begin franchising our Melrose Management HOA business – it's going to be a great opportunity for some ambitious entrepreneurs who will be able to share in the great success our company has experienced. And it will allow them to truly control their futures.

William Shakespeare said, "It is not in the stars to hold our destiny, but in ourselves." Whatever your business choice, I encourage you to be in control of your own destiny at all times - because the person that has the best intentions for you…is, of course, *you!*

About Jack

National leading property management expert Jack Hanson, LCAM, is the President and CEO of The Melrose Management Partnership based in Orlando, Florida, providing professional management services to multiple Home Owner Associations throughout the state of Florida, representing literally thousands of residents. A graduate of the University of Central Florida with a Bachelor's Degree in Business Administration, he also holds an MBA from the University of Florida as well as the designation of Licensed Community Association Manager (LCAM) from the state of Florida.

Having worked in land development for over ten years, Jack began The Melrose Management Group in 1997 after recognizing the need for start-to-finish, competent and intuitive management of single and multi-family communities under the control of the developer and builder. He then expanded his company to also include resident-controlled communities for both homeowners associations as well as condominium associations, creating a loyal following of leading Florida communities. In 2007, under Jack's leadership, The Melrose Management Group received the prestigious recognition as one of the "Top 100 Property Management Companies in Florida." Over the past 17 years he has managed over 200,000 dwellings in 500 communities and 1,250 associations statewide ranging from small to large high-rise buildings, master associations and condominiums, as well as multi-family and active adult communities.

A sought-after leading expert in the property management industry, Jack has expanded his enterprise to offer other like-minded entrepreneurs the opportunity to be mentored and utilize the proven tools and methodology that has made him radically successful. Rather than reinventing the property management wheel, those aspiring to thrive in their careers now have the opportunity to tap into Jack's vetted system that he has personally developed into a nationally recognized brand. He now teaches others how to leverage their relationships and utilize his expertise to build their own company into a multi-million dollar business.

Continuously gaining industry and media prominence, Jack has been featured on Bay News 9 and Fox News in the Florida market, as well as receiving national exposure in such prestigious publications as *New York Business Journal, Miami Herald, Reuters* and *San Francisco Business Times* as well as dozens of other high-profile business and news sources. He has also received attention from various television sites including ABC, NBC, CBS and Fox affiliates across the country.

Additional information about Jack and The Melrose Management Partnership can be found at:
www.melrosemanagement.com
or by calling his publicist directly at: 407-405-3417.